DREAM HOMES

GEORGIA

AN EXCLUSIVE SHOWCASE OF GEORGIA'S FINEST ARCHITECTS, DESIGNERS & BUILDERS

Published by

PANACHE
PANACHE PARTNERS, LLC

13747 Montfort Drive, Suite 100
Dallas, TX 75240
972.661.9884
f: 972.661.2743
www.panache.com

Publishers: Brian G. Carabet and John A. Shand
Executive Publisher: Phil Reavis
Associate Publisher: Janet Smiley
Editor: Anita M. Kasmar
Designer: Ben Quintanilla

Printed in Malaysia

Distributed by IPG
800.748.5439

PUBLISHER'S DATA

Dream Homes Georgia

Library of Congress Control Number: 2007920298

ISBN 13: 978-1-933415-02-4
ISBN 10: 1-933415-02-9

First Printing 2007

10 9 8 7 6 5 4 3 2 1

Previous Page: Bonner Custom Homes See page 63
Photograph by Danny Lee

This Page: Dawson Wissmach Architects See page 105
Photograph by Attic Fire Photography

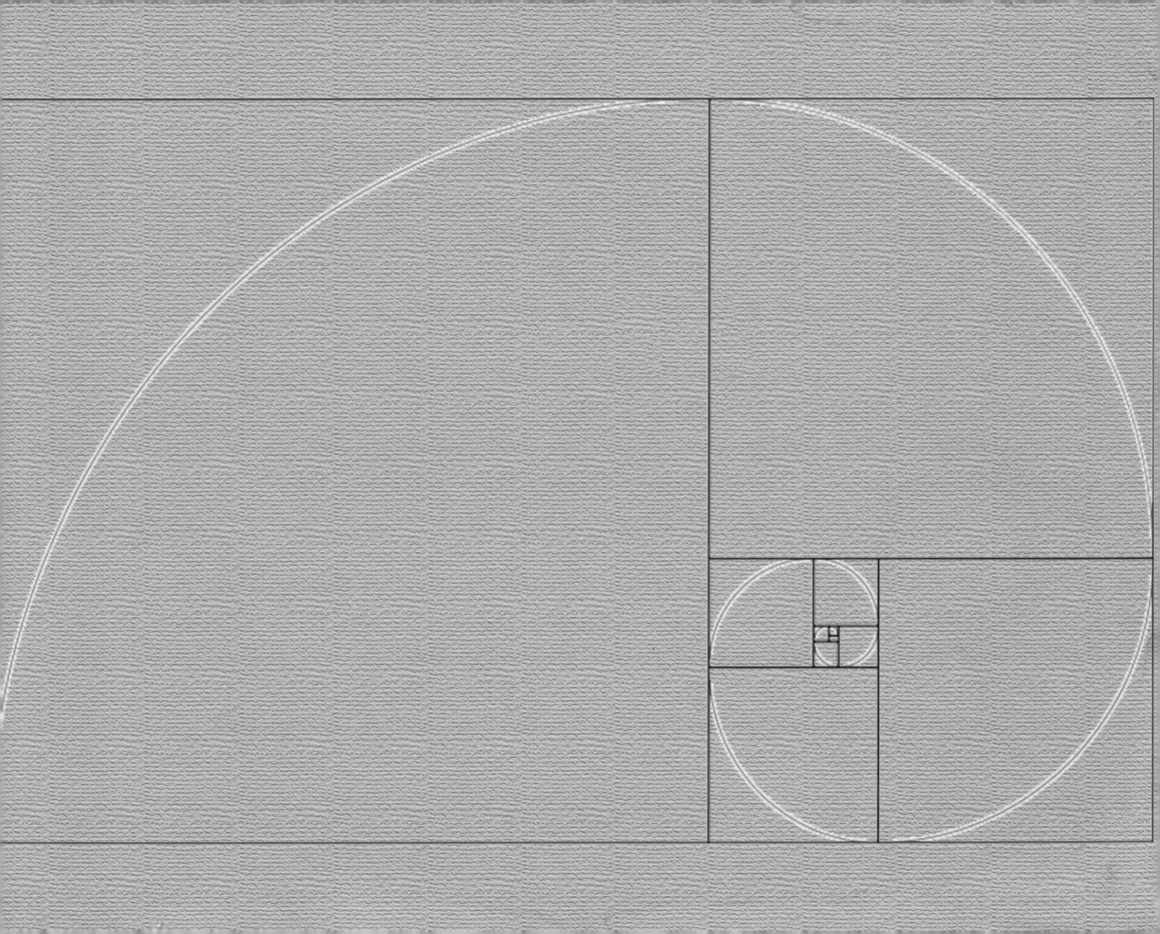

DREAM HOMES
GEORGIA
AN EXCLUSIVE SHOWCASE OF GEORGIA'S FINEST ARCHITECTS, DESIGNERS & BUILDERS

INTRODUCTION

Pak Heydt & Associates, LLC, page 219

With its beautiful North Mountains, numerous lakes, sparkling Atlantic coastline and cosmopolitan urban areas the southern state of Georgia is unique to say the least. In the pages that follow, you will come to appreciate even more the caliber of Georgia's finest residential architects and builders and their sincere dedication to classical design, historic preservation and important environmental conservation.

What you will see and read in *Dream Homes Georgia* is equal parts breathtaking and inspirational. You will visit and explore, from the comfort of your own home, the state's most exquisite properties—elegant architecture steeped in the traditional Southern vernacular. You will also experience beautiful European-influenced residences with gracious front porches, classic columns and artisan-crafted details, the sum of which truly epitomizes the stately and refined home designs for which Georgia is so well known.

Jefferson Browne Design Group, page 81

This collection of extraordinary and enduring architecture reveals the legendary luxury and tranquility of living in America's South. As is so eloquently demonstrated, Classicism with its rules of proportion, detail and precedent is very much alive and as appealing as ever. From Atlanta's famous Buckhead neighborhood to gated suburban estates and Savannah's eco-minded communities, you will discover the cultural and architectural diversity that Georgia exemplifies.

Many thanks to all of the professionals who made my journey in creating *Dream Homes Georgia* not only fun and exciting but also challenging in a delightful way. It has been a joy!

Sincerely,

Janet Smiley

Associate Publisher

William T. Baker & Associates, page 39

CONTENTS

DeLany Rossetti Construction, Inc., page 113

BWC Properties LLC, page 267

D. Stanley Dixon Architect, page 117

"Each project should begin with a precedent study to ensure that the new design will be correct in style, indigenous to its location and deeply rooted in the classical tradition."

—*David Grace, A Classical Studio*

Beecham Builders, LLC, page 45

Norman Davenport Askins, P.C., Architect, page 33

"As a true classicist, I strive to be as historically correct as possible yet adapt designs to fit current lifestyles."

—Norman Askins, Norman Davenport Askins, P.C., Architect

Cowart Coleman Group Architects, page 95

Garrell Associates, Inc., page 141

PFVS Architects, Inc., page 259

"We should be connected more to nature and our environment—bringing the outdoors in with windows and porches allows one to experience more sunlight and air flow."

—*Shawn Allen, Allen Architects, LLC*

Allen Architects, LLC, page 29

Berndsen Custom Homes, page 53

Johnson, Williams & Harris, LLC, page 179

GEORGIA

RICHARD ADAMS
CATHY ADAMS
Adams Group Builders, Inc.

Working together for 30 years, Cathy and Richard Adams share a diverse background of building commercial projects, multi-family dwellings and private residences. In 1988 they founded Adams Custom Homes, Inc. and recently consolidated their interests into Adams Group Builders, Inc., focusing exclusively on their joint passion of custom homebuilding with more than 200 custom and speculative homes to their credit. Richard, an Atlanta native, earned his civil engineering degree from Georgia Tech University and is a veteran U.S. Navy officer and construction supervisor, bringing his analytical mind and building expertise to the business. Cathy is a licensed real estate broker and an accomplished interior designer who delicately balances the financial particulars and creative design aspects of each project.

The suburban developments in which they choose to build are located throughout the north Atlanta suburbs and primarily include planned gated communities with golf course properties and exclusive neighborhoods with strong architectural guidelines. These prime areas make a perfect backdrop for the beautiful, million-dollar-plus custom

homes built by the Adams team, including the Crabapple area, where large pieces of land offer rare opportunities to build country estates with amenities including stables and riding arenas. After 30 years of success in the high-end custom market of Atlanta, they have recently expanded their operations into the thriving resort community of Highlands, North Carolina, and are ready to build to suit the most discerning clients.

Their traditional homes are designed to blend into each particular neighborhood, but always with a unique, eye-catching difference. Building in styles ranging from Country French to English Tudor or lodge-like homes using stone and cedar timbers, they often have an eclectic blend of elements. Combining brick with native stone and incorporating outdoor living areas with fireplaces, their homes complement the Georgia nature-inspired lifestyle. Collaborating with highly regarded Atlanta architects and working solely with seasoned subcontractors, the team specifically directs the design plan early in the process. Their homebuilding philosophy is to personally engage and advise each client from site selection to floor plans, decorator interiors to landscape design, keeping careful watch over the client's monetary parameters every step of the way.

TOP LEFT:
With bright sunlight filtering in, the prep kitchen of this family-friendly home offers a marble baking station, soapstone sink, textured walls and a walnut top on the island.
Photograph by Craig M. Tanner

BOTTOM LEFT:
This classic countryside manor features a fusion of exterior materials, including cedar roofing, cedar shakes, Hardi-plank siding and Tennessee fieldstone, easily capturing the essence of an elegantly relaxed lifestyle.
Photograph courtesy of Adams Group Builders, Inc.

FACING PAGE:
With sweeping golf course and lake views this terrace spa offers year-round relaxation amid the textures of natural materials such as limestone, fieldstone and cypress.
Photograph by Gregg Willett

Collecting books on architecture is Cathy's love; she is inspired by the details she sees and often incorporates notable architectural design elements into new homes to add character and personality. Adams Group Builders homes have been featured in *Atlanta Homes and Lifestyles*, *Better Homes and Gardens*, *House Beautiful*, *The Atlanta Journal* and *Builder* magazines. Cathy was featured in *The Atlanta-Journal Constitution* article featuring "Women in Homebuilding," and the firm has been honored with multiple "professionalism" awards by the Greater Atlanta Homebuilders Association, a respected group of industry peers.

Like an artist understands materials, Cathy helps individual clients during the interior finishes and selection stages, purchasing dramatic pieces such as antique mirrors, one-of-a-kind light fixtures and hand-hewn vintage beams to create special effects and ceiling arrangements of interest. Richard engineered a glass solarium as one home's focal point and Cathy complemented the room with salvaged brick to add more character to the walls. These are the distinguishing details clients can expect when entrusting the Adams Group Builders to create their personal family residence and legacy for years to come—simply put—building quality for life.

ADAMS GROUP BUILDERS, INC.
Richard Adams
Cathy Adams
6535 Shiloh Road, Suite C400
Alpharetta, GA 30005
770.410.0123
f: 770.410.0125
www.adamsgroupbuilders.com

TIMOTHY S. ADAMS
TS Adams Studio, Architects

Tim Adams, AIA, was drawn to the city of Atlanta by the prestigious reputation of the Georgia Institute of Technology where he proudly earned his Bachelor of Science degree in Architecture in 1992 and his Master of Architecture degree in 1996. During these years he readily fell in love with the architecture and flavor of the great state of Georgia as well as his wife, Kelli. After working closely with one of Atlanta's preeminent architects for nine years, Tim became professionally equipped to venture out on his own.

Tim founded TS Adams Studio, Inc. in May of 2001 and has since welcomed architect Paul Geary, AIA, as partner in their Florida office. The firm has been designing in various architectural styles for urban, suburban, mountain and waterfront properties. These styles can be seen in regions ranging from the North Georgia Mountains to Sea Island, the Carolinas, the Florida Panhandle and Keys, as well as the U.S. Virgin Islands. This growing studio is moving forward and its new custom designs include multimillion-dollar estates and primary residences as well as smaller-scale vacation cottages and second homes.

While custom residential design is the firm's primary focus, the team of 20 employees is also actively working on highly creative commercial work, including a charming winery in north Georgia, master-planned communities, office and retail spaces with lofts and exclusive town homes. Enjoying each and every client, their custom home business comes to them steadily by word of mouth. The firm's philosophy is to do their absolute best in designing, planning, detailing and execution throughout each stage of the project. This is proving to be a successful work ethic as the firm designs up to 35 custom residences annually.

TOP RIGHT:
An exemplary Shingle-style home is rooted in the quintessential Dutch Colonial architecture of the Northeast.
Photograph by Gil Stose

BOTTOM RIGHT:
The serenely simple porch of this Arts-and-Crafts-style vacation home offers an intimate place to unwind in the warmth of a natural stone fireplace surrounded by breathtaking South Carolina and Georgia mountain views.
Photograph by J. Wieland

FACING PAGE LEFT:
Interior archways flank the dining room and study of this highly detailed foyer in a formal, classical Atlanta residence.
Photograph Gil Stose

FACING PAGE RIGHT:
An American Arts-and-Crafts-style mountain home in Travelers Rest, South Carolina, offers breathtaking views of Georgia and South Carolina.
Photograph by J. Weiland

Tim is a traditionalist yet works in diverse styles of architecture based on the direction of his informed clients. He researches extensively and is prepared to design in French, English and Colonial styles, and in the Floridian vernacular exhibiting Caribbean and Low Country influences. His firm has designed private homes throughout the Southeast from English Manor-style homes in the urban areas to a sprawling 150-acre horse farm in the countryside. Tim's professional mantra is to be as flexible as possible and design well in every style. The highest compliment he has received was from one satisfied client who reiterated that the firm's architectural design truly exceeded their dreams and expectations.

TOP LEFT:
This beachfront retreat in Watercolor, Florida, is a contemporary interpretation of the coastal architectural styles found throughout Florida, Alabama and Mississippi.
Photograph by Brian Gassel

BOTTOM LEFT:
Situated on a Georgia marsh point this private residence is designed in the Mediterranean style on beautiful Skidaway Island, Georgia.
Photograph by Gil Stose

FACING PAGE:
This Greek Revival-style private residence in Duluth, Georgia, was influenced by an antebellum home located in Athens, Georgia.
Photograph by Peter Christiansen Valli

A perfectionist, Tim is a very introspective person regarding his work and never accepts mediocrity, doing the best creative work in every design. He is an avid collector of rare books on architecture and has acquired hundreds of volumes representing the best architectural styles from Europe and America. Tim references his collection periodically for inspiration and relishes gaining more knowledge rooted in historical precedence.

TOP LEFT:
This outstanding English Arts-and-Crafts-style home was inspired by the designs of renowned English architect C.F.A.Voysey.
Photograph by Gil Stose

BOTTOM LEFT:
An extraordinary American Arts-and-Crafts-style vacation home is perched on a mountaintop in picturesque Travelers Rest, South Carolina.
Photograph by J. Weiland

FACING PAGE TOP:
Custom-crafted "cattail" motif designs were skillfully cut into the wooden balcony railings of this bright white three-story waterfront home complete with lookout room in sunny Watercolor, Florida.
Photograph by Brian Gassel

FACING PAGE BOTTOM:
The comfortable and casual billiard/family room of this Florida beach home features refined woodworking from the beamed ceilings to built-in bookcases, classical mantelpiece and beautiful hardwood floors—ideal for relaxation.
Photograph by Brian Gassel

Tim is closely involved with each client from concept and preliminary design through completion of the project. He prepares hand-drawn designs based on the needs and desires of his clients. Closing his office door, listening to familiar jazz, classical or contemporary music, Tim enters his mind's eye, visualizing, pencil-sketching, refining and perfecting his design for hours, savoring the ever-evolving creative process. The studio team then solidifies the ideas with well-executed computer plans and detailed construction documents.

TS ADAMS STUDIO, ARCHITECTS
Timothy S. Adams, AIA
2969 Hardman Court NE
Atlanta, GA 30305
404.262.3499
f: 404.262.3419
www.tsadamsstudio.com

SHAWN ALLEN
Allen Architects, LLC

Listening to his clients' wishes, enhancing and elaborating upon an idea, sketching the initial concept and nurturing its metamorphosis from design to built form; it is an evolutionary process that excites Shawn Allen, AIA, with each residential design project he accepts. Providing a guiding hand in "creating the home of their dreams" is what drives this boutique architectural studio to excel. Shawn, with his associate architect-partner and wife, Laura, delivers personalized service to each and every client, bringing visions to fruition. The enterprising principal of the firm tailors each project around the client, building a symbiotic relationship and special trust between them.

Founded in 2001, Allen Architects is led by Shawn Allen, a talented and gifted Georgia Institute of Technology-trained architect. After earning his Bachelor of Science in Architecture in 1995, he had the privilege of working for preeminent Atlanta firms in both commercial and residential practices. His forte for residential design and his innate entrepreneurial spirit led him

LEFT:
An exemplary Craftsman-style home showcases signature design elements—varying materials add texture and definition to different parts of the home's exterior while a spacious front porch and balcony create outdoor spaces to be enjoyed.
Photograph by Tom Abraham Photography

29

to establish his own firm, but it was his mother's encouragement of his artistic abilities during childhood and an uncle's "stick to it" support through college that steered him into the field of architecture altogether.

Dreaming of being a pilot, his ambitious nature was evident in high school, where he won state awards for architectural drafting, actually designing homes at this young age. Today he designs second homes and vacation residences for discerning clientele; he starts with sketches and transforms them into working documents via technically advanced three-dimensional modeling software, turning dreams into reality.

The firm's specialization is English Tudor, followed by French Country and Craftsman styles. Tudors possess a classic look with historical details such as half timbering on the exterior, stonework and interesting brick patterns, weighty front doors and other early European influences.

TOP LEFT:
This organic-inspired bedroom incorporates four large windows to capture streams of morning light, which accent the gold tones of the knotty pine flooring and finishes. Natural wood finishes bring the beauty of the outdoors into the space.
Photograph by Tom Abraham Photography

BOTTOM LEFT:
The open plan of this lake residence allows for breathtaking views from the kitchen, dining and living spaces. A full-length deck along the dining area creates an outdoor place to take in fresh air and scenic water vistas.
Photograph by Tom Abraham Photography

FACING PAGE TOP:
At the moment of twilight, this residence is illuminated to show its multitude of windows and architectural details perfectly suited to this tranquil waterfront site.
Photograph by Tom Abraham Photography

FACING PAGE BOTTOM LEFT:
The family room's corner fireplace design features local fieldstone and wood. Using indigenous building materials saves energy costs associated with shipping, while the end result reflects the landscape of the region, providing a sense of belonging.
Photograph by Tom Abraham Photography

FACING PAGE BOTTOM RIGHT:
A serene sunset view overlooking the lake is spectacular from the front porch with lantern light fixture detail softly aglow.
Photograph by Tom Abraham Photography

An eclectic architect, his greatest influences include Louis Sullivan, Louis Kahn and Richard Morris Hunt. Design-driven, the firm primarily crafts new homes but is equally skilled at important historical renovations and additions for early- and mid-century homes in established Atlanta neighborhoods.

Shawn is an accessible architect who listens and understands the needs of his clients. He goes beyond essentials thinking Green; saving natural topography and integrating sustainable materials and eco-friendly products into each home, contributing to a cleaner planet as a whole. Bringing the outdoors in by adding porches and windows to experience more sunlight and air flow—integrating nature into the home—is his design signature.

Contributing to the health of the earth, this thoughtful architect loves the outdoors, enjoying hiking, camping and world travel. "We should be connected more to nature and our environment," Shawn emphasizes. Each of his beautiful home designs reflect the local topography and respect the landscape.

ALLEN ARCHITECTS LLC
Shawn Allen, AIA, LEED® AP
6239 Grand Loop Road
Sugar Hill, GA 30518
770.271.1700
f: 770.831.9700
www.allenarchitects.com

NORMAN ASKINS

Norman Davenport Askins P.C., Architect

All architects are not created equal. For more than 29 years Norman Askins has been designing classical-style residences for the people of Atlanta and the gracious state of Georgia. His love of architecture emerged at age 10 when he enthusiastically began drawing houses and buildings in his hometown of Birmingham, Alabama. This natural-born passion for drawing structures turned into a true calling and Norman made up his mind to become a professional architect.

Soon after studying architecture at the Georgia Institute of Technology and earning his bachelor's degree, he continued his education to be distinguished as one of the first Master of Architectural History graduates from the University of Virginia. He also had the post-graduate privilege of working in Pennsylvania, Colonial Williamsburg and Atlanta before he opened the doors of Norman Davenport Askins, P.C., Architect. Today, his firm has a highly trained team of architects who specialize in the Classical style.

ABOVE LEFT:
Custom-made and imported from France, this large-scale, carved limestone mantelpiece was supplied by Bo Childs.
Photograph by Brian Gassell

ABOVE RIGHT:
Inspired by European vaulted ceilings, this intimate kitchen features rough plaster walls and hexagonal antique terracotta floors. The raised fireplace and electrified antique chandelier from South America warm the room with glass-enclosed loggia just beyond.
Photograph by Brian Gassell

During his formal education, Norman's love of books moved him to become a voracious reader and avid collector on the subject of architecture, including old printings, limited editions and rarities. His large "inspiration" library includes European and American publications, and to this day Norman pages through these exquisite references for creative inspiration before each project and every night before he ends his day. He believes that this passionate obsession for beautiful books allows him to back up every design he creates with authenticity.

Norman's design philosophy is the antithesis to trendy or modern as he is a true classicist. The firm has found its mission, which is to be as historically correct as possible yet adapt designs to fit current lifestyles. Clients often want homes with kitchens as the heart, and large master bedrooms and baths to take on a luxury suite feel. His specialty is to "contemporize" older homes using a fresh interpretation, always staying true to historical precedence. He draws from American, French, Italian and English architectural styles to create homes that reflect the authentic style with exacting detail from the original period. American architects from the 1920s to the 1960s are some of his favorite Atlanta influences—including Reid, Shutze and Means—and his designs often emulate their work to exacting standards.

One quite unusual architectural project was to design an Old World wine cellar complete with natural stone walls and vaulted stonework ceilings. This complex creative challenge excited Norman because it required a team effort to develop an engineering solution as well as refined craftsmanship. It is his "can do" spirit and the highly technical

RIGHT:
The adjacent loggia has stucco walls and ceilings, checkerboard travertine floors, antique columns from Palm Beach and custom steel windows and doors by Rod Gibson, renowned blacksmith. The pergola features antique columns from India flanking a path to the wall garden.
Photograph by Brian Gassell

ABOVE:
Plaster walls and ceilings with massive, antique adzed beams from an old building in North Carolina, supplied by Bo Childs.
Antique French terracotta tile floors, leaded glass mahogany windows made in France by Asselin. Living room appointed by
interior decorator Joane Askins.
Photograph by Brian Gassell

FACING PAGE:
An almost cube-shaped space in the front of the home, this private reading room is upholstered in vibrant, red silk with
Provence toile touches.
Photograph by Brian Gassell

knowledge and experience of his architectural team that get the job done every time.

His firm is known for designing new, traditional homes as well as a high percentage of seamless renovations because Atlanta residents prefer to stay in their existing homes and believe in renovating versus relocating. He has designed homes for families referred from generation to generation and for several members in the same family. Through word of mouth, Norman's architecture is in exceedingly high demand and his home designs command premium real estate prices. You can often see his design work featured in national magazines including *Southern Accents*, *House Beautiful*, *Veranda* and others.

It is the people element that makes Norman's work so rewarding. He loves his clients, contractors, craftsmen, engineers, decorators and tradespeople because in the end it takes a team effort to create a one-of-a-kind home, renovation or addition. Most of all, he has a genuine good time during the process of each design experience and intends to never retire from the business. To Norman, being an architect is fulfilling because people can enjoy living in their dream home for years and it feels so rewarding to be appreciated by each client. Working hard with an honest promise to please people is his tried and true philosophy, it is this strong American work ethic that is perhaps the secret to his success. Norman Davenport Askins' stately, legendary home designs stand the test of time and are the epitome of architectural classicism in America.

NORMAN DAVENPORT ASKINS, P.C., ARCHITECT
Norman Askins
2995 Lookout Place
Atlanta, GA 30305
404.233.6565
f: 404.233.0395
www.normanaskins.com

WILLIAM T. BAKER

William T. Baker & Associates

Imagine being a multi-degreed business man with a passion for architecture and an uncommon combination of intellect and creativity. Tapping into his many talents, William T. Baker has become one of Georgia's most beloved, award-winning residential designers. Combining creative talent with a Master of Business Administration from Emory University, Bill has an edge when it comes to understanding the delicate balance between fine design and budget.

The school of business and a focused attitude is only one half of Bill's success story. Working in the construction field with framers, carpenters and craftsmen early in his career gave Bill an appreciation for attention to detail and the art of fine craftsmanship. He founded William T. Baker & Associates in 1985 as a boutique shop and now designs great American homes in Georgia and throughout the United States.

Photograph by William Waldron

Timeless, classic designs and well-proportioned homes are Bill Baker's hallmark. Personal service, attention to detail, and an unerring sense of proportion and scale are integral parts of each and every design. Hand-carved stonework, elaborate millwork, plaster cornices and trim, iron fabrication and slate roofs are some of the most impressive details incorporated into his designs. To Bill, each home is a blank canvas for the craftsman and a perfect place to show artistry within a residence. He has also found that integrating antique architectural details into a home design is another interesting way to bring the artful past into the present.

In Bill's words, "classicism never goes out of style" so creating a home for today's needs utilizing time-proven principles is his biggest design challenge. His solutions are custom residences that meet current lifestyle needs by interpreting historic styles for modern living. The real art is to retain historic integrity and create the total design with true-to-form exteriors as well as original interiors that function well for the American family. From four-car garages to flowing floor plans, his designs are practical for daily life while delivering the aesthetic goals of his well-informed, discerning clientele. Homes designed by his firm are claimed to be "family friendly" and his plans age beautifully, possessing a timeless look.

Photograph by William Waldron

Photograph by William Waldron

Photograph by James Lockheart

Inspired by 20th-century American architects including Shutze, Reid, Bottomley, Means, Jones and Staub, Bill Baker designs his classic residences with reverence to those who have come before but with a sensitivity to modern living. In 1993 Bill was honored as an exemplary design practitioner in the classical style when he received the coveted Arthur Ross Award for Architecture in New York City. This recognition elevated Bill as a nationally-acclaimed designer and garnered him invitations to participate in decorator show houses, which benefit charitable organizations such as the Susan G. Komen Breast Cancer Foundation and the Atlanta Symphony Orchestra. His residential work has been published in national magazines including *Veranda, Southern Accents* and *House Beautiful*. Bill's first book, "New Classicists," was published in 2004 and features residences from the first 20 years of his practice. It has become a sought-after book for architectural students and home design aficionados both in the United States and abroad. The book has also been translated into Mandarin and is widely distributed throughout Asia.

Bill's visionary thinking and foresight to see design trends before they appear in the mainstream is what sets him apart from his contemporaries. He works closely with each client from concept through completion, providing his creative expertise in residential design every single step of the way.

WILLIAM T. BAKER & ASSOCIATES
Bill Baker
78 West Wesley Road NW
Atlanta, GA 30305
404.261.0446
f: 404.261.0549
www.wtbaker.com

Photograph by James Lockheart

HARRY BEECHAM
BRENT BEECHAM
ROB BEECHAM

Beecham Builders, LLC

Building an unsurpassed reputation for more than 75 years, four generations of Beechams have worked in Georgia. Harry Beecham Sr., who made his mark in Florida's plastering and stucco business during the 1920s and 1930s, moved to Atlanta in the post-war boom to build homes throughout metro Atlanta. Everett Beecham, the second generation Beecham builder, continued in the family business, building in DeKalb and Clayton County through the 1950s. Harry Beecham, Harry Sr.'s grandson, founded Beecham Builders in 1958, becoming the cornerstone of today's Beecham Builders, LLC. With a degree in building construction from Southern Polytechnic University, his lifelong passion has been to build homes using solid, time-tested construction techniques.

The tradition of building was ingrained in Harry's sons and Brent joined with his father after graduating from the U.S. Air Force Academy, where he studied general engineering. A Gulf War veteran, he is the company's financial professional, handling the matters of money pertaining to every building project with an "honor code" philosophy. Rob Beecham later joined the firm after graduating from Theological Seminary and serving for 11 years as a minister.

He brings a sense of community to all that Beecham Builders produces and has taken the family business into the realm of philanthropy with fundraising for non-profit organizations and the cultural arts, most notably the Alliance Theatre and Atlanta Symphony Orchestra. His strong materials knowledge makes him an important advisor to each client during the selection of products and finishes throughout the building process.

The firm is headquartered in Roswell's Historic District. With a team of experienced project managers, contractors and skilled tradesmen, they draw on the resources of each other, meeting the highest quality standards during each multimillion-dollar project. Building up to 12 custom residences per year, the Beechams personally attend to each client along the way, and with avid father-son pilots leading the firm, they have the natural ability to see the big-picture perspective as well as focus on the fine details.

Beecham Builders takes great pride working with many of Atlanta's prominent architects, staying true to Atlanta's architectural roots from the 1920s and 1930s. The classical architecture, character and beauty intrinsic to Atlanta is evident in each custom residence.

LEFT:
This stylishly appointed master bathroom features a soaking tub, his and hers vanities and a domed ceiling. The builder strived to use natural materials to create an inviting environment for the owner.
Photograph courtesy of Beecham Builders

FACING PAGE:
The elegant kitchen is the focal point of the English manor home with antique beams, pediments, custom cabinets and Subzero and Wolf appliances. The home was featured in several local magazines and was the site of a charity fundraiser.
Photograph courtesy of Beecham Builders

Working with the best design firms in Atlanta, a recently-built Beecham Builders home was recognized with the prestigious Sub-Zero International Kitchen Design award for excellence in kitchen design. This dream kitchen was built for the 2003 Alliance Theatre Christmas Show House. With a flair for dramatic interior details, Beecham built a 30-foot-high domed ceiling constructed of solid wood framing and plaster in the 2005 Christmas Show House. In addition to professional awards, Beecham Builders' luxury residences have been published in *Atlanta Homes & Lifestyles*, *The Atlanta Registry* and *Today's Custom Home* magazine.

The Beecham family is dedicated to the art of custom residential building, principally in metro Atlanta and the North Georgia Mountains. Possessing a strong family work ethic with four generations of perfecting their craft, their custom dream homes are known and loved by their sophisticated clientele and the architecturally rich city of Atlanta.

BEECHAM BUILDERS, LLC
Harry Beecham
Brent Beecham
Rob Beecham
1158 Canton Street
Roswell, GA 30075
678.566.6651
f: 678.566.6653
www.beechambuilders.com

BILLY BENEDICT
Benedict Homes, Inc.

From managing investment portfolios to building a portfolio of homes for more than 25 years in the urban Atlanta Buckhead and Sandy Springs communities, Billy Benedict is one creative talent, constructing multimillion-dollar classical custom residences and renovations for discriminating clients. A fifth-generation Atlantan, Billy, and his wife, Snow, an accomplished real estate broker and his inspiration, live and work in the town they truly love.

Knowing the neighborhoods so well and also having a large family of four brothers nearby, Billy is at home building in the upscale Atlanta market. After receiving his liberal arts degree from the University of North Carolina and earning his master's degree in business administration from Georgia State University with honors, Billy started his first career in the stock market as an investment management professional. Deep in his heart he always knew his first passion was building—ever since he designed and built his first home in 1972, where he still resides today. He enjoyed the process so much that he made a career change midstream and proudly founded Benedict Homes, Inc.

One of Billy's unique professional talents is his ability to conceptualize and provide effective solutions including workable floor plans, appealing interiors and attention to interior details. He can look at a piece of property and immediately know which floor layout will be most effective and start hand-drawing plans. He is very sensitive to the flow of traffic in a home and makes sure families will have a plan that fits their specific lifestyle and needs. Partnering on projects with Atlanta's preeminent architects, Benedict Homes are built with a client's vision in mind, carefully modeled after classical architecture and always rooted in historical precedence. His new constructions fit seamlessly in context with important architectural styles of an established neighborhood and look as though they have always been there.

One special project the firm built was an indoor swimming pool on the terrace level of a beautiful in-town estate. This was an engineering challenge and required exceptional attention to heating and air conditioning requirements as well as aesthetic considerations. Working with seasoned subcontractors and experienced superintendents makes each building project a smooth success; and their showcase of elegant, solidly built homes and timeless renovations are proof of this process.

LEFT:
The welcoming Craftsman-style brick and Pennsylvania fieldstone residence greets guests through the charming arched entry porch—topped by a cupola and weathervane.
Photograph by John Umberger

FACING PAGE TOP:
Overlooking the swimming pool, this elegant living room is anchored by a limestone mantel with surround. The light, spacious feeling is created by 12-foot coffered ceilings, oversized French doors with transoms and wide-plank hardwood flooring.
Photograph by John Umberger

FACING PAGE BOTTOM:
A state-of-the-art gourmet kitchen boasts tall custom cabinetry with a sophisticated antique white finish and polished marble countertops for a refined European touch.
Photograph by John Umberger

This award-winning builder relies on personal referrals and has always had clients come to him with great enthusiasm, since his reputation is well known in the Atlanta area. He has a following of loyal clients because he consistently works hard to meet and exceed their expectations.

An intense personality and enthusiastic sportsman, Billy Benedict has played a good game of tennis and is now an avid golfer who shows his perfectionist qualities on and off the course. Being a custom home builder provides him with the opportunity to solve challenging problems and achieve a visible end result, ultimately pleasing each client and seeing them realize their dreams.

BENEDICT HOMES, INC.
Billy Benedict
3012 Wellington Court NW
Atlanta, GA 30339
770.431.0231
f: 770.431.0232

JON BERNDSEN
Berndsen Custom Homes

Berndsen Custom Homes provides a wealth of building and design experience, along with a determined resolve to ensure each project far exceeds the customer's expectations. Together, the Berndsen team has established a company renowned for its attention to detail and professionalism, and incomparable high quality.

With a solid background in large commercial building and a degree in construction engineering from the acclaimed Auburn University School of Architecture, Jon Berndsen moved to Atlanta in the mid-'80s and made his transition into custom residential building. With his passion for superior quality workmanship, he entered a niche market building exceptional, historically accurate classical homes in Atlanta.

A residential builder for more than 20 years and a certified general contractor since 1986, Jon Berndsen wholeheartedly involves himself in each unique project. Jon works closely with his project managers and subcontractors to ensure

Before

continuity in quality, schedules and budgets. All craftsmen utilized in the construction process are masters of their respective trades and share an unyielding commitment to excellence.

Few builders can offer the beautiful, complete package which Berndsen Custom Homes delivers to its clients. Moreover, few homes exemplify the high quality construction of a Berndsen residence, finely crafted with luxury, refinement and character. With more than 150 notable projects completed, Berndsen's satisfied clients have discovered the true meaning of "home." This is why so many referrals come from former and existing clientele, and why so many clients are repeat customers.

The Berndsen staff offers building experience in a vast range of design styles, from Old World/Traditional, Colonial, French and Italian Renaissance, Country French, Craftsman/Cottage, Tudor and Gothic Revival, Georgian and Regency, to log and timber-framed. Whatever the architectural style, Berndsen Custom Homes researches and studies the architectural details and techniques of that style, crafting a home worthy of praise and admiration.

TOP LEFT:
A limestone balustraded front entry with fountain welcomes you to "La Dolce Vita," a classic post-Italian Revival estate home that tastefully incorporates subtle Baroque details.
Photograph by Berndsen

BOTTOM LEFT:
A renovation, this French Country style home was originally a modest 1950s' ranch house. This home has won awards for its remarkable transformation. Architecture by William T. Baker.
Photograph by Berndsen

FACING PAGE:
Classic balustrades, gardens and bluestone terraces lead you to the pool of this Italian Renaissance estate. Axial symmetry is an important element of this architecture. Landscape Architecture by Land Plus Associates.
Photograph by Berndsen

There are only a select few who actually understand the classical principles and have demonstrated a history of quality practice. It is for this reason that the firm was chosen to become one of the founding members for the Southeast Chapter of the Institute of Classical Architecture and Classic America. The ICA/CA was established to promote the value of classical and traditional design in creating built environments of the highest quality. As a founding member, Jon is honored to be a part of this exclusive organization underscoring his work as a true classicist.

Renovations are also a big part of the work that Berndsen Custom Homes provides. Over the years, the highly skilled team has restored some of Atlanta's most prestigious estates. Projects include those originally designed and built by such noted and heralded classicist architects as Phillip Shutze, Neel Reid, Clement Ford, James Means and Lewis Edmund Crook Jr. Berndsen Custom Homes has also been honored to be the chosen builder for some of Atlanta's prominent, current-era architects for their own personal residences.

Their remarkable residences have been featured in *Traditional Home*, *Better Homes and Gardens*, *Atlanta Homes & Lifestyles*, *Veranda*, and *Southern Living* magazines. Eight of their projects have won the prestigious OBIE Award from the Greater Atlanta Home Builders Association for both best new home and best renovation.

LEFT:
Berndsen Custom Homes also focuses much attention to details outside of the homes it builds. Here, a classic limestone lion's head gracefully returns water to this fountain.
Photograph by Berndsen

BERNDSEN CUSTOM HOMES

Jon Berndsen, ICA/CA, CGC, CR
201 Allen Road, Suite 404
Atlanta, GA 30328
404.303.7272
f: 404.303.7223
www.berndsencompany.com

ABOVE LEFT:
Specialty rooms are an integral part of Berndsen homes. Wine cellars, paneled libraries, home theaters and billiard rooms are commonly featured.
Photograph by Berndsen

ABOVE RIGHT:
This formal library features an Italian hand-carved limestone mantel, paneled walls and bookcases crafted from old-growth French oak imported from Versailles, and antique hand-hewn oak beams.
Photograph by Berndsen

NATHAN BONHAM
Bonhambuilt, Inc.

A self-taught artist and lover of architecture, Nathan Bonham's passion is ever-present in his fine art of custom home building. He grew up surrounded by the arts, thanks to his father, a renowned American sculptor. Nathan's father was his first mentor and he continued to apprentice in art studios throughout his youth. This creative upbringing inspired Nathan to become a professional painter but it was his knowledge of how to use materials that catapulted him into the business of building custom residences since 1996.

He studied the craft in-depth, transitioning from painting and sculpting to building. Nathan started working on older houses, restoring Victorians in Toronto by working on beautiful millwork and plaster as his first job in the business. He and his wife, Cathy, moved to Georgia in 1992 where Nathan ran a sheet rock company. It was this on-the-job experience, ability to analyze and solve visual-spatial problems and a love of architecture that impelled him to become a custom builder.

It was Nathan's natural eye for design, bringing harmony and symmetry to a project, understanding size and proportion that brought him to success. He is a builder who can identify problems, recommend solutions and offer aesthetic control. Clients work in tandem with Nathan during the course of the building process, in which he literally draws on the walls every step of the way to convey what is needed to perfect a room. His floor plans and exterior designs always reflect the work of a solid draftsman.

Nathan's specialty is period home construction—developing designs in keeping with the vernacular of the style and being true to architectural roots. It is adhering to historical precedence that makes a Bonhambuilt custom home one that stands the test of time. From American Shingle and Tudor Revivals characteristic of the eastern seaboard's Golden Age of homes, to classical southern Georgians and progressive Contemporary designs, these styles are all in the palette of possibilities.

TOP LEFT:
Integrated beautifully into the wooded home site, this classical custom residence was designed in collaboration with Jim Klippel from Garrell Associates, Inc.
Photograph by Adamo Photography

BOTTOM LEFT:
This traditional English Tudor kitchen features high ceilings dramatically detailed with distressed beams and bull-nosed plaster soffit to create an Old World charm.
Photograph by Adamo Photography

FACING PAGE:
An impressive view from the terrace steps reveals artistic, custom-welded, wrought-iron scrollwork railings and a curvilinear suspended balcony.
Photograph by Adamo Photography

The art of building custom residences is always rewarding to Nathan but one home is special in that regard. Nathan designed a handicapped-accessible home for an executive confined to a wheelchair. His challenge was to create a home with features that did not look like an access home so Nathan created a home with a custom driveway at one level with the entry, a custom shower, sink areas and counters to allow for complete mobility. The home was awarded the "Easy Living Home" seal of approval for meeting program criteria.

A recent project required blending the contemporary tastes of a client within an upscale traditional architecture community. Nathan made it happen and solved a technical challenge to create a two-story round room suspended by cantilevered support structures to essentially "float" in the space. He also designed a sweeping, circular staircase to connect the two floors exemplifying form and function, a great artist's signature and the Bonhambuilt custom home trademark.

BONHAMBUILT, INC.
Nathan Bonham
201 Saddle Creek Trail
Alpharetta, GA 30004
770.844.7393
f: 770.886.4482

JERRY BONNER
RHETT BONNER
Bonner Custom Homes

Father and son team Jerry and Rhett Bonner are a duo dedicated to building dream homes for their respected Atlanta clients. Born in Griffin, Georgia, Jerry moved to Atlanta in 1978 and founded Bonner Custom Homes. He was building since 1969 after earning his degree in engineering from Southern Tech and serving in the U.S. Army. Rhett joined the family business after graduating college at Samford University in Alabama, learning the trade directly from his dad.

Both are passionate about custom residential building, and the combination of his perfectionist son coupled with Jerry's "can't say no" attitude means that they serve their clients with utmost attention. The firm builds primarily in metro Atlanta, the historical Buckhead community, as well as North Georgia Mountains and Alabama. They are recent members of the Greater Atlanta Home Builders Association.

LEFT:
The rear façade of this custom Italian villa in Atlanta showcases Old World workmanship and authentic reclaimed barrel-tile rooftop imported from Europe.
Photograph by Erica George Dines

Jerry and Rhett are accomplished custom homebuilders and true relationship-builders. The energetic team shares the passion to move the process from vision to reality and always finds a way to build it right with the utmost integrity. Excellence is what their professional, celebrity, pro-athlete and executive clients can expect from this legendary builder; the bond of trust between Bonner Custom Homes and each client is immeasurable.

Jerry has a passion for travel and he visits Europe frequently. His philosophy is to build family homes with the same sense of permanency as seen in Europe. That says it all because a Bonner Custom Home has a sense that it has always been there, fitting seamlessly into an established neighborhood. He loves traditional architecture as in French country homes, English manor and Tudor cottages. European homes were built with permanency in mind and he loves refining new homes with an American influence retaining the solid, Old World feel. Masonry walls and authentic building techniques, the true roots of good architecture, are incorporated into each custom home.

LEFT:
This dramatic aerial view of a sprawling Atlanta estate shows the central 47,000-square-foot English manor residence amid formal gardens and a beautifully designed, park-inspired setting with related amenities.
Photograph by Keith Rocke

FACING PAGE LEFT:
An impressive groin-vaulted gallery connects the primary reception rooms of this classical home featuring high-quality Hope's steel doors opening to the terrace garden with custom leaded-glass panels executed by Pat Vloebergh.
Photograph by Erica George Dines

FACING PAGE RIGHT:
The golden antique oak-paneled library with charming demilune desk and work station overlooks the home's restful rear garden.
Photograph by Erica George Dines

Working with the most renowned architects in the Southeast, Jerry finds building the most rewarding outlet for his creative side. The firm employs specialized cabinet makers and interior woodwork craftsmen who have worked with Jerry for many years, so the level of fine workmanship is incomparable—befitting his high-profile clientele. When you enter a Bonner Custom Home there is a feeling of timeless character and tradition. However, he prides himself on creating the most "uniquely different" homes in the traditional style.

Custom Homes magazine recognized Bonner Custom Homes with the coveted 2005 Pacesetter Award for its innovative ideas for creating an expansive 40-million-dollar custom home in north Georgia. Their select custom residences have been featured in *Atlanta Homes & Lifestyles, Better Homes and Gardens, Southern Homes, Veranda, Southern Accents, Success, Trends* and *Home and Living* magazines.

TOP LEFT:
This middle Georgia residence's rear façade is designed and built to reflect historical precedence, integrating Texas limestone throughout the loggia and terrace.
Photograph by Danny Lee

BOTTOM LEFT:
A middle Georgia home's main entry hall boasts a spectacular flying staircase—designed by Timothy Johnson—which gracefully ascends from highly polished stone floors imported from Jerusalem.
Photograph by Danny Lee

Jerry was only 12 years old when he began working with his uncle, a commercial contractor in Griffin. He taught Jerry about basic construction, bookkeeping and the client service aspects of being a builder. With gratitude for this major influence in his life he has passed all of these inherited qualities on to Rhett as they move the firm to the next generation of Bonner builders.

RIGHT:
The view through the foyer entrance archway shows a sweeping circular staircase with decorative wrought-iron details and ancient stone floors imported from Europe.
Photograph by Danny Lee

It is the creativity of building that Jerry thrives on, and he loves serving his Georgia clients who speak his language of quality architecture and high-end home design. His international travel takes him to his favorite places, especially one architectural antiques shop just outside of Paris. "Origines" is a resource he searches for one-of-a-kind architectural elements to incorporate into custom home designs such as 1,000-year-old columns, impressive antique doors and roof tiles, leaded windows and recycled stonework from authentic European structures. These are the details that make a house a home. Whether visiting Europe or touring the homes of former American presidents, he is a history buff who keeps the art of craftsmanship alive, bringing inspiration to building custom private residences.

Bonner Custom Homes has taken the building process to a new art form with the secret ingredient being unlimited passion. Jerry never wants to retire because he is totally fulfilled expressing his creativity through his work, creating custom residences that fulfill the lifelong dreams of his clientele. For seasoned building expert, Jerry Bonner, the business is his greatest pleasure and his greatest pleasure is his business.

TOP:
This charming English cottage-style home with natural stone and earth-toned brick exterior is capped by a reclaimed, genuine clay tile roof from England.
Photograph by Brian Gassel

BOTTOM LEFT:
The corner roofline shows the unique reclaimed clay-tile roof from England.
Photograph by Brian Gassel

BOTTOM RIGHT:
Rustic brick work and natural stone details create a rural, countryside look to this English cottage home.
Photograph by Brian Gassel

FACING PAGE:
The homeowners' breathtaking vista is enjoyed from the rear terrace on axis through the elegant swimming pool and ellipse pond with fountain, terminated by a classic Palladian-style folly.
Photograph by Keith Rocke

BONNER CUSTOM HOMES
Jerry Bonner
Rhett Bonner
269 Lawrence Street NE
Marietta, GA 30060
770.423.0249
f: 770.423.0301
www.bonnercustomhomes.com

SCOTT BROWN
Comfort Home Builders

The discipline, drive and dedication of a former U.S. Army Black Hawk helicopter aviator may be the reason why this Gwinnet County builder is considered one of the best in the new custom home construction business. Major Scott Brown grew up with construction in his veins, his father a residential builder and grandfather a notable electrical and plumbing sub-contractor—family greatly influenced him in his youth and he chose the noble profession for himself.

Scott believes that having been a man of honor in service to his country has taught him to "pay attention to details," an admirable trait that is critical to successful home building and an essential part of the military culture. This parallel has served to be instrumental to the growth of this second-generation firm for nearly a decade. With the philosophy and heartfelt company motto, "It's not just a house, it's your home," the number one goal of every project is to celebrate the essence of the client. Scott's firm works sincerely to capture the sophistication and style that defines its clients' character to create a space that will be loved, cherished and most of all, lived in for years to come.

A member of the Greater Atlanta Home Builders Association and designated Certified Professional Home Builder, Scott and his five-person office include superintendents and project managers who work together as a team for their respected clientele. The team prides itself on working extremely close with each client as it custom designs and carefully constructs what is to be the single most significant investment of a lifetime.

The firm's approach to customer service is second to none and the team creates a comfortable atmosphere right from the start. With a detailed timeline and scheduled meetings at every construction phase, clients have the opportunity to take an active role in the building process from beginning to end.

Inventing his own tried-and-true "checklist" methodology for all phases of the process, from digging the foundation to exterior materials and interior finish selections, as well as audio, security and central vac systems, his detailed list is a proven tool utilized by staff, contractors and the homeowner clients. In this way everyone is prepared for the process ahead, the project stays on track and surprises are prevented to better meet and exceed expectations.

LEFT:
The floor-to-ceiling stacked stone fireplace is an eloquent response to Georgia's chilly evenings.
Photograph courtesy of Comfort Home Builders

Earth Craft Certified, the firm also integrates standard "comfort" features in the majority of its custom homes to ensure steady temperature control with proper sealing, insulation and house wraps to keep out unwanted heat and moisture. Seventy-five percent of Scott's work as a general contractor is throughout suburban Georgia, but the breathtaking waterfront communities of the Florida Panhandle are also home to his expanding residential and commercial work.

The preferred residential style most often requested by clients has a traditional European influence with Old World flair, yet his classic homes incorporate leading-edge technology, including home theaters, steam rooms and whole-house networking known as "Smart Home" technology, whereby temperature, motion detection devices, garage doors and even ovens are accessible and can be controlled remotely via the Internet at the push of a button. Technology expertise and high-quality craftsmanship is the firm's hallmark and working with an established cadre of contractors makes all of the pieces join together perfectly like a puzzle.

TOP RIGHT:
This custom home theater is replete with state-of-the-art system components.
Photograph courtesy of Comfort Home Builders

BOTTOM RIGHT:
Ideal for formal and casual entertaining, alike, this bar area is handcrafted of mahogany.
Photograph courtesy of Comfort Home Builders

A full-service firm, Scott brings in an interior designer to help clients during the finishes/color selection process and to put the final touches on each signature home. Landscape architects are brought into the mix to enhance the home's exterior, add curb appeal and bring each home to life; especially for custom homeowners as well as for speculative home developments. Homes feature refined and graceful living spaces that flow seamlessly from one grand area to the next—impressive rooms with ornate trim work, beautiful views and wonderful architectural details.

The remarkable residences built by this reputable firm are found in some of northeast Georgia's most coveted estate communities— replete with club houses and amenities—such as Gainesville's Deer Creek Crossing, Buford's Hidden Falls and Lanier Springs near Lake Lanier. Many of the properties feature picturesque wooded homesites as well as pristine natural settings amid scenic waterfalls—perfect backdrops for Scott's well-crafted custom

TOP LEFT:
This southern traditional kitchen's custom cabinets and professional-grade appliances set the mood for modern convenience.
Photograph courtesy of Comfort Home Builders

BOTTOM LEFT:
Everyone enjoys this keeping room's cozy ambience. Residents and guests enjoy visual interaction with the chef without getting in the way.
Photograph courtesy of Comfort Home Builders

single-family homes. Refined comfort, extraordinary luxury and exquisite elegance are qualities consistently experienced in a Comfort Home Builders home. The team's mission is to strive to provide unparalleled service and quality, valuing honesty, fairness, integrity and teamwork. Expecting these same standards of excellence from its contractors, tradesmen and vendors is paramount to offer the highest degree of professionalism during the complex building process.

The most memorable client compliment that Scott relays is perhaps the most telling: "This was by far the easiest process—smoother than any other home I have ever built." His secret to success is threefold: To not reinvent his already proven "checklist" process, to stay on top of knowledge and integration of new technology and to maintain ongoing, interactive communication between all parties.

RIGHT:
The rear kitchen stairs lead to the children's suite with playroom.
Photograph courtesy of Comfort Home Builders

An adventurous spirit and family man to the core, in his leisure time, Scott enjoys the extreme sport of motocross racing with his young son. It is with equal intensity and a passionate energy that Scott and his team work to exceed a client's vision and reach the finish line with a beautiful final product.

RIGHT:
Completely custom in design and build, the curved glass-block shower provides both practicality and timeless beauty.
Photograph courtesy of Comfort Home Builders

FACING PAGE LEFT:
Exposed beams in the vaulted ceiling, hardwood flooring and the gas fireplace give this formal living area warmth and character.
Photograph courtesy of Comfort Home Builders

FACING PAGE RIGHT:
This master bath oasis includes a large bathtub with jets as well as a full-body shower graciously sized to accommodate two.
Photograph courtesy of Comfort Home Builders

COMFORT HOME BUILDERS
Scott Brown
958 McEver Road Extension, Suite B-3
Gainesville, GA 30504
770.532.8299
f: 770.532.8992
www.comforthomebuilders-ga.com

JEFFERSON BROWNE

Jefferson Browne Design Group

"A well-designed home is a portrait of its owner," says Jefferson Browne, the principal of Jefferson Browne Design Group, a firm of more than 25 years with projects ranging throughout North America. "It is like a song you grew up with, a place that takes you back, a place that physically demonstrates where you came from."

For Jefferson, superb architectural design must evoke emotion. It must connect to the viewer's very soul. By resurfacing forgotten memories, it promises to forge new ones. After all, nothing can articulate a dream, a personality or even a long-buried childhood more effectively than architecture. It is humanity's sole means to mold the world. And, as such, no design aspect is too small for consideration. Each space, each decoration, each angle should reflect the owner's experiences. In Jefferson's mind, it is not enough that his art must imitate his clients' lives, but that his art must embody their lives: Do they crave morning sunrises with flooding light? Do they envision dining alfresco under the stars? What do they love? What are their dreams? These are the questions to which excellent architecture must find answers.

Jefferson's design philosophy is a continued quest to balance innovation and renovation. With each project, he reinvents the past to serve the future: historical precedents meet modern demands—time-honored materials marry technological advances—classical ideals meld with contemporary ideas. "Tradition is not an end to itself," Jefferson continues to stress. "But, rather, it represents the building blocks of an artistically correct foundation." Consequently, in his hands tradition does not limit or constrain. Rather, it provides an opportunity to create richer and more poignant architecture.

By emphasizing flow, proportion and historical precedents, Jefferson crafts authentically styled projects that not only build upon the immediate and surrounding areas, they enhance them. His signature design style, Shingle-style, utilizes classical forms: chimneys, porches and natural materials are, simultaneously, historically accurate and timely. They are familiar and warm. They are inviting yet elegant. Indeed, this is more than mere attention to minutiae. It is the process of coaxing wonder-filled details from commonplace spaces, of finding the delightful within the dull; a place for meditation, an inspiration-worthy view or an architectural styling that contextualizes who his clients are.

TOP RIGHT:
Too many homes are merely beautiful architectural shells—every interior detail must continue the family's visual story.
Photograph by Jefferson Browne

BOTTOM RIGHT:
The casual basement contrasts with the more formal upstairs living room, but both spaces remain connected by lush textiles and rich colors.
Photograph by Jefferson Browne

FACING PAGE:
Using the owner's deep love of Charleston as a springboard, traditional Southern forms were exploited to highlight the property's spectacular views.
Photograph by Jefferson Browne

Where other designers fit clients into their visions, Jefferson grows his visions around the firm's clients. The result is a family's visual story, a physically articulated reflection of the home's inhabitants. And yet through his characteristic interplay of light, color, texture, historical precedents and natural materials, each home needs little introduction as a Jefferson Browne creation. Instead, they speak for themselves.

These are the results of a design process filled with discovery. A client's needs must not be confused with designer-manufactured wants. A home must not modify, but add to a client's life. Good design dignifies a family's day-to-day experiences. And, moreover, a good designer understands these experiences. Jefferson has participated in every aspect of the home industry from building and design, from laborer to master carpenter, job foreman to project manager—his diverse job experiences have provided invaluable knowledge of a home's internal workings and, more importantly, of a homeowner's needs. Ultimately, Jefferson seeks to create more than just beautiful structures; he crafts the environments in which well-lived lives take place. He firmly believes that homes are the "stage" of life. They provide the backdrop to humanity's inherent drama—the needs, the wants, the dreams. And, as such, the residence must never interfere with the drama itself.

LEFT:
The room's strong architectural boundaries of crown moulding and pillars contrast with the curved, overstuffed furniture and soothing colors.
Photograph by Jefferson Browne

FACING PAGE LEFT:
Blurring the transition between indoor living spaces and outdoor living spaces is essential for year-round living.
Photograph by Jefferson Browne

FACING PAGE RIGHT:
Jefferson created a sense of place and connection for his clients by bringing in elements reminiscent of their childhoods in Portugal.
Photograph by Jefferson Browne

Such commitment to livable environments and beautiful spaces can only come through the most implicit understanding of his clients' lives. Indeed, Jefferson shapes the character and style of his projects through the meticulous cultivation of personal relationships with his clients. If tradition is his design's lifeblood then trust is its backbone. Homes are the most intimate arena of architecture. And through the careful examination of each family's goals, associations, backgrounds and even fears, Jefferson unearths the clients' ideal design and style. In order to preserve this heightened aesthetic, Jefferson is careful to select only projects that will ignite his team's imagination. Capitalizing on the firm's tightly-knit staff, Jefferson allows their enthusiasm and spirit of collaboration to turn every client's home into a dream home.

Many firms would stagnate under such close insulation, but almost solely by word of mouth, Jefferson's has quietly flourished. Indeed, the typical Jefferson Browne Design Group client is accepted through referral alone. This approach, however, has by no means kept Jefferson restricted. His project portfolio ranges from a hunting camp for terminally ill children in Grand Rapids, Michigan, to coastal homes in Maryland to guest lodges in Maine and beach retreats in Florida. The studio's custom residential design work is evident in Georgia, Maine, Delaware, the Carolinas, Maryland, Florida and Michigan.

LEFT:
The tower's strong architectural statement is softened by natural materials and colors.
Photograph by Jefferson Browne

FACING PAGE:
To take advantage of the property's many vistas, Jefferson curved the home. Consequently, every elevation provides a unique view.
Photograph by Jefferson Browne

This practice is a labor of passion. For Jefferson, home design represents one of the most rewarding spheres in which to work. And, in the face of today's global-village homogenization, it is becoming an increasingly important mission. These are more than mere buildings. America's homes represent the final symbols of arrival. They are birthrights and dreams—sometimes years in the making. From inception to completion, a Jefferson Browne home strives to symbolize not only its owners, but what all of us endeavor to realize within ourselves. Ultimately, superior architecture should not only reflect who the client is today, but also who they aspire to become.

RIGHT:
By situating courtyards, and sunrooms or even pools near kitchens, dining rooms and bedrooms, Jefferson provides seasonal living spaces without hampering the main structure.
Photograph by Jefferson Browne

FACING PAGE:
Another example of Jefferson's commitment to Green architecture, this home is a LEED-certified Silver design.
Photograph by Jefferson Browne

JEFFERSON BROWNE DESIGN GROUP
Jefferson Browne, AIBD, CPBD
Peachtree City, GA
770.632.9545
f: 770.632.9544
www.jeffersonbrownedesigns.com

JAMES COTTON
DAN MATTOX
Builders II

Combine an industrial engineering degree from Georgia Tech with a master's degree in real estate and business from Georgia State University and you have James Cotton, entrepreneur and champion builder. Add third-generation contractor and partner Dan Mattox to the mix of 25 years and you have Builders II. Together they share common credentials as past presidents in the Greater Atlanta Home Builders Association as well as CABO certification, which confirms their practice of professionalism.

This is the story of two of Atlanta's most talented builders, true traditionalists and experts in the classical architectural style characteristic of renowned in-town neighborhoods. James lives in Buckhead, which keeps him close to clients where they build new custom residences and perform historically precise renovations. The Builders II team has been voted Builder of the Year, has won numerous accolades from its peers and recently received the Atlanta Urban Design Commission award

LEFT:
This stately residence embodies classical style and symmetry even from the backyard garden view. Herringbone-pattern brickwork, a natural slate patio, and French doors with wrought-iron railings give the home Old World charm while the reflecting pool creates a tranquil feeling.
Photograph by James Lockhart

for best infill house of 2005. This award acknowledged one custom home that integrated naturally into the residential architecture characteristic of Druid Hills, a community designed by Central Park's famed Frederick Law Olmsted. Working directly with the most respected classical architects in Atlanta, the firm executes plans to exacting detail and in alignment with historical precedence.

Custom building is an art form and it takes time, patience and talent to create a new home that looks like it has always been an intrinsic part of an established, historic neighborhood. Building in Buckhead is their specialty, an elegant, understated community with many residents who have lived there for several generations. Serving this small, close-knit community is what gives James Cotton and Dan Mattox the joy of shepherding people through the process of building a custom home and communicating their client's vision to loyal subcontractors. Effective listeners, they help their clients through every decision during the process, presenting construction steps in an organized way with ample lead time. Their unique open-book system of accounting allows clients to share in project knowledge and reap cost-saving benefits.

Builders II custom homes have been featured in national publications including *Southern Living*, *Atlanta Homes* and *Lifestyles*, *Veranda* and *Builder/Architect* magazines. The team takes pride in building custom homes and providing customer service of the highest level because they know that it is a family affair. Building for someone's family life, creating a very personal space that will delight the homeowners for years to come and watching the home become a realized dream are all important to James and Dan.

Their own mutual respect speaks to their honored client-builder relationships and many have turned into lasting friendships in the process. Building beautiful custom homes with total customer satisfaction in mind is their company philosophy and they deliver it all with a trusted handshake and a smile.

BUILDERS II

James Cotton
Dan Mattox
120 West Wieuca Road, Suite 200
Atlanta, GA 30342
404.303.1104
f: 404.303.1516
www.builders2.com

ABOVE:
An English Manor home showcases classical form and exacting details from the natural slate roofline and gables to the limestone-framed windows. The Pennsylvania bluestone walkway with gravel and cobblestone drive integrates into the natural wooded landscape.
Photograph by James Lockhart

FACING PAGE:
Classic and elegant details of intricately carved millwork, bas-relief mantel, stylized columns and graceful archways inspire a living and dining room. Leaded glass windows and French doors bring filtered sunlight in from the garden retreat.
Photograph by James Lockhart

GERALD D. COWART
W. SHEDRICK COLEMAN
Cowart Coleman Group Architects

ABOVE:
This sun-drenched combined living and dining area is an inviting gathering place for family and friends at the "Tree House" in Palmetto Bluff, South Carolina.
Photograph by Jeff Cate Photography

FACING PAGE:
This corner house sets the stage at the entrance to Palmetto Bluff's Wilson Village, epitomizing gracious Southern living with welcoming wraparound porches.
Photograph by Jeff Cate Photography

While finishing his master's thesis at Georgia Tech, Gerry Cowart, AIA, came across the following quote by Sir John Soane, circa 1795: "We must be intimately acquainted with not only what the ancients have done, but endeavor to learn from their work what they would have done. We shall, therefore, become artists … not merely copyists." Soane's words made an indelible impression on Cowart, one that remained with him long after he finished graduate school, to launch his successful career in architecture. Inspired by a deep respect for the past and a love for the natural environment, Gerry founded Cowart Coleman Group Architects alongside partner W. Shedrick Coleman, AIA. Together they have created Southern architecture, derived from its context and history but embodying a modernism and artistry that respects historical evolution.

The firm's Savannah, Georgia, location provides the perfect setting for Gerry and Shedrick's aesthetic penchant. The partners feel lucky to practice their craft in the beautiful and pristine environs of Georgia's Barrier Islands and along the Carolinas' coastal estuaries. Equally fortunate is the region—the firm's great concern for preserving

historic Southern sites while promoting environmentally sensitive, contemporary development and design has brawn the attention and accolades of peers and clients alike. Widely published in national and regional publications, the firm's work has garnered numerous awards for sustainable design, 35 AIA awards for design excellence and seven awards for historic preservation.

Shedrick credits the firm's success in part to its site planning and analysis. His vast experience has taught him that devoting as much time as necessary to gaining an in-depth understanding of the building's environment is key to successful architecture. The architects thus commence each project by visiting the site to glean inspiration for each unique design. All projects are sensitive to environmental factors—sun angles, shade, breezes, drainage and views. Yet Gerry states that each site resonates differently with his sensibility, instilling in him a special understanding that informs and ultimately improves the architecture's design. Time and again, clients have remarked that the firm possesses an inherent talent for integrating structure and site. Gerry cites his respect for nature and the immense pleasure he

gets from discovering the nuances and intimacies of a place as the factors that lead him to design homes that look and feel native to their environments.

Along with sensitivity to the site's aesthetic qualities, the firm practices Leadership in Energy & Environmental Design (LEED). Gerry and Shedrick bring a passion for sustainability and habitat preservation to their projects. Their reverence for nature has led to their efforts to save indigenous trees, a practice that has become a hallmark of the firm's work. Gerry has become an amateur botanist over the years, gathering a wealth of scientific knowledge about the characteristics and needs of different area species. This understanding helps him best plan sites to work in harmony with existing trees, fostering their health and further growth. The firm's "Outfitter's Cottage" exemplifies the partners' capacity for designing in harmony with trees. Surrounded by salt marsh and nestled in a pocket of live oaks on the bank of the Okatie River, the site provided the perfect opportunity for preservation. Shedrick and Gerry carefully mapped all of the trees and their low-hanging limbs, before designing the 6,000-square-foot retreat to capture the exceptional views while remaining sympathetic to the vulnerable environment.

TOP RIGHT:
The "Outfitter's Cottage" residence exemplifies how a home was designed in concert with nature—protecting graceful age-old tree limbs on property in Oldfield Plantation, South Carolina.
Photograph by Rebecca Thaden

BOTTOM RIGHT:
This spacious living area features expansive windows in "Outfitter's Cottage," offering a tranquil backyard view of the native live oaks beyond.
Photograph by Rebecca Thaden

FACING PAGE:
Beautiful twilight reflections mirror the pristine natural setting surrounding "Outfitter's Cottage," with a river view in Oldfield Plantation, South Carolina.
Photograph by Rebecca Thaden

Saving trees is just one of Cowart Coleman's sustainable measures. Gerry and Shedrick feel it is their obligation to reduce the need for fossil fuels in the homes they design—so much so that they have accepted the challenge to use half of the energy they did five years ago and little or no fossil fuels by 2030. Their method for achieving these goals is threefold: First, their intimate knowledge of the regional climate, vegetation and terrain allows them to design homes that make use of each via passive solar energy, natural ventilation and natural lighting. Second, the firm's buildings conserve the energy they do use with high-performance windows and high-efficiency insulation, and state-of-the-art heating and cooling systems. Third, the partners advocate the use of new alternate technologies, such as solar electricity and geothermal heat.

The firm also employs recycled materials in its home designs, such as that for the "Foster's Heart Pine Hunting Retreat." For it, Gerry located a cotton mill that was to be demolished and salvaged the wood, remilling it for the home's flooring, wall paneling and moulding. Select pieces were reserved for the home's front door, fireplace mantels and kitchen cabinetry, and the firm saved even the smallest remaining pieces for use in later projects. Recycling not only

RIGHT:
Southern solar shade and eco-friendly rainwater cistern are features of the "Tree House" in Palmetto Bluff, South Carolina.
Photograph by Jeff Cate Photography

FACING PAGE:
The Palmetto Bluff "Tree House" features an authentic copper roof that is very sustainable and ultimately easy to recycle. Natural-finished, reclaimed cypress siding was used throughout.
Photograph by Jeff Cate Photography

eliminated the need for new timber, but by buying in bulk, it cut costs in half—a definite benefit to the client. The result was an extraordinary contemporary home that paid homage to history while supporting the environment—and the client's budget and lifestyle.

While context and sustainability profoundly impact the firm's work, the partners maintain that the client is essential to each design. The firm has developed a well-tested, successful approach to the interview process. But Gerry and Shedrick have found that the most effective method to discover clients' needs, tastes and ways of life is to visit them in their homes. After careful examination of the site, the partners enjoy visiting with clients for a weekend, sketching ideas and intuiting the clients' visions for their home. While this may seem an extreme measure, it epitomizes the partners' shared commitment to create architecture that others will love as much as they.

LEFT:
Recycled heart pine planks line the floors, walls and ceilings of the rustic living room in a residence on Brays Island, South Carolina.
Photograph by Joseph Lapeyra

FACING PAGE LEFT:
A screened porch fireplace features a hand-hewn recycled beam mantel in this charming home in The Ford Plantation, Savannah, Georgia.
Photograph by Jeff Cate Photography

FACING PAGE RIGHT:
Relaxed outdoor living is at its finest amidst the graceful trees in "Outfitter's Cottage," Oldfield Plantation, South Carolina.
Photograph by Rebecca Thaden

COWART COLEMAN GROUP ARCHITECTS

Architects • Land Planners • Interior Design
Gerald D. Cowart, AIA, LEED® AP
W. Shedrick Coleman, AIA
107 East Gordon Street
Savannah, GA 31401
912.236.1372
f: 912.236.9960
www.cowartgroup.com

NEIL DAWSON
RICHARD K. WISSMACH

Dawson Wissmach Architects

Entrepreneurs with high energy, this young dynamic firm embodies the essence of creativity and exhibits a healthy competitive spirit throughout; a team motivated by its founding principals, one being an avid tennis player and the other a water sports enthusiast. Rick Wissmach, AIA, and Neil Dawson, AIA, joined forces in 1999 after meeting as associates in a Savannah commercial firm; this meeting was fortuitous and within months they decided to embark on a partnership establishing Dawson Wissmach Architects, offering more than 30 years of combined design experience.

Their flourishing studio is located in the heart of the historic district in a renovated 150-year-old building on The Factor's Walk overlooking the Savannah River. In a space that epitomizes its architectural style and philosophy, the firm retained original elements of the old cotton warehouse including vintage heart pine floors and exposed brick walls. They integrated new,

LEFT:
This one-room-deep second home affords each space views of the lake and 100-year-old live oak hammocks beyond.
Photograph by Attic Fire Photography

contemporary elements, including skylights and birch woodwork, making the office space within this mixed-use building remarkably fresh and visually clean.

This contemporary attitude is at the core of the design process. In each residential project the firm undertakes, it incorporates contemporary elements—choice of materials, positioning of spaces, or the simplification of details—to fundamentally traditional homes. By pushing this "transitional" architecture that blends the classical with contemporary, their signature style was formed. Rick received his formal training at the University of South Florida where he earned a Master of Architecture degree, while Neil earned master's degrees in both architecture and business administration from the University of Illinois. Their open-concept studio structure promotes total collaboration, focusing on what unique talents and skills each individual brings to the process. This insightful business philosophy has resulted in the synchronized team it is today, made up of 16 people working from a position of strength who are extremely passionate about what they do.

TOP LEFT:
Wood timber beams and posts and rustic appointments are fitting in this carriage house whose design was inspired by the historic outbuildings of old Southern plantations.
Photograph by Attic Fire Photography

BOTTOM LEFT:
Expressed timber floor framing placed below the "hay loft" (kids' sleeping loft) is the fully functional kitchen.
Photograph by Attic Fire Photography

FACING PAGE:
The siting of this home as well as its configuration was orchestrated to capture multiple pocket views through the woods to the golf course beyond.
Photograph by Attic Fire Photography

Being located in Savannah offers a special niche opportunity for the firm, as this coastal region draws people from the Northeast and Midwest in search of beautiful second homes. The region's residential developments revolve around traditional Southern forms that maximize picturesque coastal settings. This context has influenced the firm's designs and has resulted in these luxury custom homes becoming the studio's trademark. Designing residences that range from $1 million to $5 million dollars, each home, though at first glance is primarily traditional, incorporates contemporary, even playful elements. The firm advocates the exploration of fresh ideas for the marriage of familiar, classic forms with modern functionality.

In the earliest days of the Savannah firm, the two partners became intensely involved in the redevelopment of the historic downtown area. Renovation work was a springboard and the firm gradually developed an expertise in custom residential projects in private developments, including The Ford Plantation, Palmetto Bluff and Colleton River, as well as designing mixed-use urban buildings with residential loft spaces. Licensed to practice throughout Georgia, Florida, the Carolinas and West Virginia, the team studies the local vernacular of each region and creates contextual designs that incorporate locally derived materials appropriate to the established architectural heritage.

RIGHT:
Concrete stained floors, galvanized wall panels and exposed trusses complement this "guys' hangout" where sporting, fishing and outdoor grilling are among the favorite activities.
Photograph by Richard Leo Johnson

FACING PAGE LEFT:
Maximizing space and efficiency among refined appointments was fundamental in this elegant carriage house kitchen.
Photograph by Richard Leo Johnson

FACING PAGE RIGHT:
The design captures the open flow of living: from kitchen to dining to living. Spaces are open yet individually articulated.
Photograph by Richard Leo Johnson

Rick initiates the design process with in-depth client meetings to establish the direction of the project. He is the firm's lead designer, and is primarily responsible for preliminary design concepts. Clients can expect to be actively involved in the design process.

The firm utilizes a "design lab" where clients and designers interact to provide clear decision-making that sequentially leads the team through the design process. Neil ensures that final construction documents will be exacting down to each meticulous detail, adhering to building codes and technical standards, with a degree of flexibility in mind. By engaging each client from start to finish and making them an integral part of the process it guarantees a better design and a "no surprises" experience.

The firm is respectful of the beauty within the natural context of the region. They believe in carefully siting each home in order to seamlessly integrate it into its environment. Many of their designs are based on traditional vernacular and neoclassical styles, yet all involve the use of sustainable materials, eco-friendly systems and proven high-performance technologies. To its credit, the firm designed the first ever LEED-certified mixed-use building constructed in Savannah

TOP LEFT:
This perspective captures the juxtaposition of open lawn to carefully nestled carriage house gently placed among forest trees on this 29-acre site bordering the marsh.
Photograph by Attic Fire Photography

BOTTOM LEFT:
Unique configuration of site required an unconventional approach to building forms in order for key living spaces to fully take advantage of pristine lake views.
Photograph by Attic Fire Photography

FACING PAGE:
Marriage of old and new: modern conveniences of guest home in the historic forms of barn and dovecote are reminiscent of an old Southern plantation.
Photograph by Attic Fire Photography

in 2003 and to date they continue to be a recognized leader in environmentally sensitive design. The firm has also earned recognition from the Savannah Chapter of the AIA as well as multiple Preservation Awards from both the Georgia Trust for Historic Preservation and the Historic Savannah Foundation.

Rick and Neil have complementary skill sets and their partnership provides a perfect balance of art and business. Their driving passion is to achieve a "timeless" design aesthetic fit for modern living, and the firm is renowned for this creative approach. Committed to Savannah, taking a cue from historical precedence and adding a modern sensibility to its design work, the firm is enhancing its clients' lifestyles while adding to the architectural splendor of Georgia and America's South.

DAWSON WISSMACH ARCHITECTS
Neil Dawson, AIA, LEED® AP
Richard K. Wissmach, AIA
12 East Bay Street
Savannah, GA 31401
912.201.0111
f: 912.201.0143
www.dwarch.com

JIM DELANY
JOE DELANY
JEROME ROSSETTI
DeLany Rossetti Construction, Inc.

ABOVE:
An elegant Potomac Avenue residence showcases the central formal staircase with intricate decorative carving and hand-wrought iron railing.
Photograph by Barbara Brown Photography

FACING PAGE:
Rays of morning sunlight glimmer across a classical swimming pool in this serene, sophisticated courtyard of a Wood Valley Road residence.
Photograph by Barbara Brown Photography

Born into families of professional home builders, "Building on Tradition" is the underlying foundation of this Atlanta firm specializing in custom renovations, new residences and development. Brothers Jim and Joe DeLany together with Jerome Rosetti founded the firm and formed a partnership in 2001 after the trio had already gained a wealth of experience in the construction business since the mid-'80s. Jerome had expertise in new custom housing and development and Jim and Joe were adept in large-scale renovations, remodeling and additions. As a newfound firm they bring more than 60 years of collective building experience to their upscale in-town Atlanta market.

The three men grew up in the renowned historic neighborhoods of Buckhead and Brookhaven and became fast friends during their high school years. They continued their education at the University of Georgia, becoming college roommates while earning their bachelor's degrees. Attracted to the residential construction companies that their fathers had started, they have grown passionate about their own business of custom renovations and home building. On the development side, they have expanded into building luxurious multifamily townhomes as well.

The firm is an active member of the Greater Atlanta Home Builders Association and participant of Energy Star and Earth Craft House. An innovative team, they have completed the first Green home in the Southeast to exemplify U.S. Green Building Council standards and have received a Leadership in Energy and Environmental Design rating for this progressive residence built in 2007. The Ecomanor home operates on solar electricity, geothermal heating and air conditioning and has tankless water heaters as well as a water reclamation system. Local Atlanta clients are requesting this type of construction more frequently as it is becoming the wave of the future and a trademark for the firm.

Living and building in the communities that they enjoyed as children, the DeLany Rossetti Construction team has an in-depth understanding of its clientele, the history of the area and the superior standards of excellence that must be upheld when building on prime urban property. The firm delivers on its promise of high attention to historic details, from seamlessly manufacturing and matching existing 80-year-old trim work to building a new custom residence that looks as though it is an original structure blending into the architectural context of the community. Working with loyal, respected contractors, the firm ensures expert craftsmanship and a commitment to enduring quality; it exclusively uses authentic materials to stay true to historical precedence and maintain the look and feel of the neighborhood.

Working with the crème de la crème of Atlanta architects, the firm has a mutual respect for its peers. Thriving on its affinity for building relationships from clients to architects, contractors to vendors, the team has a passion for people and its 100-percent referral business speaks for itself. This compatible team is honest and hard-working with a backbone of integrity. They infuse the complex building process with a relaxed attitude each day while working with and for friends taking the fine art of custom home renovation, building and developing to an unprecedented level.

DELANY ROSSETTI CONSTRUCTION, INC.

Jim DeLany

Joe DeLany

Jerome Rossetti

397 Armour Drive, Suite 200

Atlanta, GA 30324

404.969.0358

f: 404.969.0360

www.drconstruction.net

ABOVE LEFT:
An aerial view of solar roof panels is featured in this eco-friendly custom home—a residence designed to be completely solar-powered and built to meet Green codes.
Photograph by Barbara Brown Photography

ABOVE RIGHT:
This Ecomanor home's family room is spacious, airy and entirely solar-powered for environmentally conscious living.
Photograph by Barbara Brown Photography

FACING PAGE TOP:
A private residence at Wood Valley Road welcomes guests in a traditional formal dining room—a prime example of exquisite detailing with high ceilings, paneled walls, unique wooden doors and hardwood floors.
Photograph by Barbara Brown Photography

FACING PAGE LEFT:
This well-appointed library features a graceful, arched and recessed niche with classical moulding details and custom built-in bookshelves and cabinetry.
Photograph by Barbara Brown Photography

STAN DIXON
D. Stanley Dixon Architect

ABOVE:
This geometric and linear iron rail with brass finial surmounts the curvaceous forms of the treads and volute below.
Photograph by Brian Gassel

FACING PAGE:
Nestled in Atlanta's famed Buckhead neighborhood, this residence recalls an 18th-century French Provincial estate.
Photograph by Brian Gassel

In Atlanta, architect Stan Dixon, AIA, is captivated by the fact that Atlanta can be sophisticated and urban, and at the same time embrace neighborhoods of distinct character and defined space.

The successful commingling of modern theory and historic aesthetic gives Stan's work a fresh vision, which imparts an easy gentility to the classical nature of his inspiration. Atlantans are known for their love of style, and it is little wonder that the firm's use of historical precedent and understanding of place and context have garnered special notice. Working with historic materials and antique salvage, each project remains true to the period of inspiration, whether it is Greek Revival, Georgian, Mediterranean or the European country houses. Finding the inherent beauty and texture of earthen brick, stone, slate or wood adds distinctive warmth to each home. Stan incorporates finely crafted windows and doors, shows sensitivity to historic patterns and details and communicates an understanding of overall scale and proportion, while at the same time he accommodates for a contemporary lifestyle and allows for a contemporary aesthetic.

Stan Dixon is a graduate of the architecture program at the University of Tennessee, Knoxville. Although he began his professional career in commercial design, he quickly realized his passion for residential design. As a child he loved visiting historic homes and beautiful old neighborhoods; those houses and neighborhoods are what brought him to architecture. After 17 years, Stan has become an influential member of the architectural community, and has become known as an architect that creates classical homes that complement the fabric of Atlanta's architectural heritage.

The study of classical design has been restricted to a handful of programs throughout the country and in general has been considered the domain of the architectural historian. Many architects, upon graduation, choose to practice traditional design, but few pursue the rigorous course required to become a classicist. Stan has been privileged to be mentored by one of the most highly respected classical architects in the South. During those years he took his apprenticeship very seriously. From the guidance of his mentor to the study of historical precedent, his membership in professional organizations such as the National Trust of England, The Classical Institute of Architects and his involvement in preservation organizations, he has made it a practice to take advantage of every opportunity to learn. Travel continues to play an extremely important

RIGHT:
With its custom, carved limestone mantel and antiqued, hand-waxed oak paneling, the library of this residence provides a warm and inviting atmosphere.
Photograph by Brian Gassel

FACING PAGE LEFT:
Sunlight dapples across the parged brick façade, carved limestone entry and Vermont slate roof in the forecourt of this residence.
Photograph by Brian Gassel

FACING PAGE RIGHT:
The flooring in this kitchen is antique French oak. The island was modeled after a French pastry table.
Photograph by Brian Gassel

role in shaping his design aesthetic. Stan is an alumnus of the Attingham Summer Study in England, an exclusive course for professionals in architecture and the allied arts. He drew upon this opportunity to examine the architectural social history of the historic house in Britain; its gardens, landscapes and decorative arts. World travel to Europe, Asia, the British Isles and Eastern Europe has provided additional inspiration and continues to inform his vibrant and lifelong passion for good design.

Good design and sensibility of place and scale have become the cornerstone of the five-person firm, D. Stanley Dixon Architect, established in 2005. Careful to keep the firm small and with a philosophy centered on excellence, Stan's highest priority is to create an environment that fosters an open exchange of creative ideas. Every successful project is a collaboration between the architect and client, interior designer, landscape architect, craftsmen and builder. All must participate in shared goals with a shared sensibility.

Stan's goal is to fulfill the client's wishes as well as create meaningful architecture that brings delight to their family, friends and community. The intention is to build something that adds to its surroundings and possesses a lasting and appropriate beauty. This beauty is not determined by its size or budget, yet is determined by its character, quality and appropriateness—to age gracefully and continue to delight.

RIGHT:
Dramatically sited in the mountains of North Carolina, this vacation home affords panoramic views of mountain ranges and nearby Lake Toxaway.
Photograph by Brian Gassel

FACING PAGE:
The proposed garden elevation for a residence in Atlanta was designed to resemble a manor house with English Palladian and Regency influences.
Rendering by Jonathan LaCrosse

The firm's success has garnered recognition throughout Atlanta and it boasts projects in areas such as Palm Beach, Charleston, Nashville, Charlotte, Birmingham, and the North Carolina mountains. For Stan, architecture is a process that begins with site selection and analysis of context and environment. This is followed by a rigourous design process and continues through construction and the craftsmen that make it all happen. "We are attuned to the preferences of each client and operate with the intention to clarify the design goals, communicating them effectively to our craftsmen so as to bring those goals to fruition." Above all, Stan conveys "We work hard and love what we do."

RIGHT:
With hand-waxed wood trusses and integrally colored plastered walls, the great hall is no less impressive as it is intimate, recalling Baronial Halls of old England.
Photograph by Brian Gassel

FACING PAGE:
The exterior materials, comprised of Alabama and Tennessee fieldstone, Vermont slate roofing, oak trim, and antique york stone paving, were chosen for their ease of care and ability to age gracefully in this mountainous environment. The Lutyens-style chimney and antique chimney pots from England define the flavor of this home.
Photograph by Brian Gassel

ABOVE:
The Beechwood woodwork of this stair hall was milled from reclaimed barn wood. The bleached and waxed finish gives a sense of mellow timelessness and comfort.
Photograph by Brian Gassel

RIGHT:
With heavy timber framing and steel windows, the connector leading from the main house to the garage resembles a porch that has been converted to interior space.
Photograph by Brian Gassel

FACING PAGE LEFT:
An artfully crafted arched door and handcrafted iron railing provide a whimsical touch while overlooking the great hall.
Photograph by Brian Gassel

FACING PAGE RIGHT:
Looking out over the entry porch, the larder is as decorative as it is functional, displaying an elegant collection of English creamware and baskets while concealing typical pantry items.
Photograph by Brian Gassel

D. STANLEY DIXON ARCHITECT, INC.
Stan Dixon, AIA, ICA
2300 Peachtree Road NW, Suite C-101
Atlanta, GA 30309
404.574.1430
f: 404.574.1435
www.dsdixonarchitect.com

KIRYA J. DUNCAN
Design Evolutions Inc., GA

Growing up in historic Natchez, Mississippi, on the banks of the renowned river, Kirya Duncan was born into an area rich in architecture. His mother noticed his passion and talent for drawing and encouraged Kirya to pursue drafting classes during his high school days at a local trade school. Taking her advice, he enrolled in mechanical drawing, learned the basics of residential design, entered a statewide competition and took first place—the impetus that led him to the profession of custom home design.

He studied drafting and design at Hinds Community College in Raymond, Mississippi, and went on to attend the University of Southern Mississippi in Hattiesburg, majoring in architectural engineering and becoming a member of Kappa Alpha Psi Fraternity, Inc. Mentored by one of his professors, Kirya knew what he was meant to do. He moved to Atlanta in 1995 and worked for acclaimed residential designer David Loftus from Archival Designs, and under his strong influence passionately became a residential designer exclusively applying his diligent efforts to the art and business of custom home design.

Opening his own residential design studio in 1999, Kirya is principal and sole designer. His clientele come to him by referral through builders and developers and he has a strong working relationship with his fellow professionals. His designs have been acknowledged in the industry as he is an annual participant of the Live Design Competition sponsored by the Southern Builders Show, where he and his award-winning designs have been recognized and showcased in *Today's Custom Home* magazine.

Specializing in all new construction, Kirya has been designing private residences in the suburbs, namely Stone Mountain, Conyers, Lithonia and Loganville, as well as some urban projects in Atlanta. His firm has designed custom homes in Georgia, Alabama, Mississippi, Tennessee and Michigan as well as in Canada, developing both stock homes and custom homes. He develops them one of two ways: either creating custom designs and converting them to stock plans; or creating stock plans, incorporating the latest trends within parameters from developers and then providing an elevation to fit into the look and feel of the area. Kirya enjoys the respect and recognition from peers—and their willingness to work closely with him—from developers to builders to interior designers, all of whom regularly refer clients to him for custom home designs.

TOP LEFT:
White custom cabinetry with black granite countertops set at various heights and a contrasting wood island create visual interest in this inviting gourmet kitchen.
Photograph by S. Waite

BOTTOM LEFT:
The tasteful and practical kitchen design exemplifies a functional food preparation triangle with ample light and sufficient workspace to create family meals with ease.
Photograph by S. Waite

In reference to Kirya's residential design preference, he embraces a classical style based on principles of proportion and scale learned from Greek, Roman and other examples of pure classicism. He is not typecast in any one style and his breadth of knowledge and expertise allows him to design residences from a small Craftsman bungalow to a massive Tudor, French Country or Colonial, and most recently, Tuscan-inspired Mediterranean villas. One unique project is a commissioned rustic log home design for a sloped, wooded property in Ellijay, nestled in the foothills of the North Georgia Mountains. All of Kirya's work demonstrates classical characteristics; just like the splendid architecture of his Natchez hometown—a timeless presence surrounds every custom residential design he touches. Kirya's single-pointed focus is to pay homage to historical design principles yet adhere to today's lifestyles so the design will continue to work generations later—this noble goal has been realized for more than 15 years.

RIGHT:
A red brick Georgian-style residence with cedar shake shingle detailing complements the home's traditionally designed exterior.
Photograph by S. Waite

ABOVE:
Classic proportions are the basis of this symmetrical exterior design—an arched entrance flanked by columns gives this stately residence a timeless curb appeal.
Photograph by T. Sigley

FACING PAGE:
An open staircase gives a sense of spaciousness and the stained wooden banisters with pure white painted posts and railings add striking contrast and classical interest.
Photograph by S. Waite

To Kirya, the most rewarding aspect of being a residential designer is working with clients and participating in the evolution of their dream home. Kirya's professional philosophy is simple yet profound: form follows function. A time-honored and proven design concept, he believes one must first understand the functionality of the home, and then the form will naturally evolve and take place. When he meets with each client personally, he delves deeply into their lifestyle, determines their needs and logically executes plans based on the way they are going to live in the home.

Kirya loves the diversity of the people in Atlanta because they bring in new influences giving him the freedom to design in a variety of styles. Traveling to destinations across the United States for added design inspiration, each trip becomes an architectural "tour," and he has acquired a substantial library for reference, including his latest treasure, A Field Guide to American Houses by Virginia and Lee McAlester. A family man first and foremost, this self-proclaimed workaholic has a 24/7 dedication to residential design and it shows.

DESIGN EVOLUTIONS INC., GA
Kirya J. Duncan, AIBD
2140 McGee Road, Suite C-140A
Snellville, GA 30078
770.978.4043
f: 678.638.1073
www.designevolutions.com

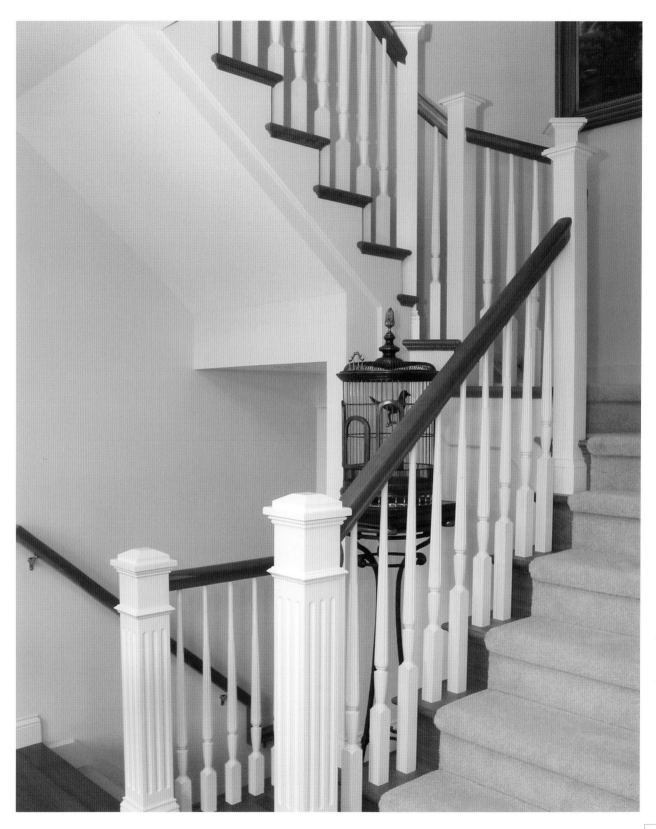

WILLIAM S. EDWARDS

Edwards Architecture, Ltd.

The commissions of Edwards Architecture may be found throughout the Atlanta area from historic Buckhead, Brookhaven and Midtown to north Atlanta and Sandy Springs. Across the state many of the firm's custom residences are situated along coastal Georgia and in Thomasville stretching north to the Georgia mountain and lake region. Over the past 20 years Bill Edwards and his team have also produced projects outside of Georgia—including Texas, Alabama, Florida, Tennessee and the Carolinas. Diversity and uniqueness are expressed in each project, influenced by location and context.

Based upon client desire and requirement, the firm's designs range from traditional to contemporary, all with a modern sensibility for today's living. From French- to English-inspired homes and coastal cottages, to rustic residences in the mountains, Bill and his firm maneuver within a broad range of architectural styles, always timeless and classic. The majority of their custom homes exhibit relaxed charm and character reflecting regional and strong American influences.

ABOVE LEFT:
The entrance hall of this contemporary home was created to exhibit a commissioned sculpture by Arnoldo Pomodoro. The central light-filled atrium runs the depth of the home culminating with a 20-foot cantilevered stone terrace with spectacular views overlooking the Chattahoochee River.
Photograph by Mary Ann Ramsey Smith

ABOVE RIGHT:
The sunroom of this Atlanta home serves as a gathering place for family. Walls and ceilings of wood, antique pine flooring and beams create a warm and inviting setting. The guest house, viewed through the windows, anchors the private garden and lawn.
Photograph by John Umberger

FACING PAGE:
The breathtaking view was integral in the siting and design of this second-home retreat in northern Georgia. High ceilings with a full window view of the lake and mountains beyond offer a relaxing focal point.
Photograph by William Waldron

Born and raised in Thomasville, Georgia, Bill was greatly influenced by the noteworthy residential architecture of the area, especially plantation homes and historic districts, which spurred his early interest in architecture and drawing. Bill attended the Georgia Institute of Technology, where he earned his undergraduate and graduate degrees from the respected College of Architecture. During college he traveled throughout Europe, studying and observing firsthand the landmark architecture he had examined in textbooks; an experience that still inspires him today.

Executing a large number of renovations of existing residences as well as designing new custom homes, his firm strives to build lasting relationships with its clients, which often leads to new opportunities. Bill delights in being referred to by his clients as "my architect," and that alone is a gratifying reward. The greater compliment is being granted the opportunity to design and work on subsequent projects with the same clients. As principal of the firm, Bill is in touch with his clients from the first interview through design and construction. He has a natural and professional talent of interpreting what his clients imagine, transforming their vision into reality. One client couple enthusiastically expressed that although they love to travel and have traveled extensively, there is no place that rivals their own home.

Bill is a passionate architect and trusted advisor to his informed, urbane clients. Whether they are a young family forecasting needs for the future as their family grows, or "empty nesters" planning a lake house to be enjoyed with friends, children and grandchildren, his firm is a sincere partner in the process of creating dream homes. To Bill, it is not only about walls and windows; it is about meeting the needs of his clients through the creation of uniquely functional and beautiful architecture.

EDWARDS ARCHITECTURE, LTD.
William S. Edwards
2974 Hardman Court NE
Atlanta, GA 30305
404.869.2443
f: 404.869.2446
www.edwardsarchitecture.com

DAVID FROST
MARK FROST

David L. Frost Builders, Inc.

A thriving family-owned building business is the direct result of a dedicated father who instilled this solid work ethic to his sons: "Work hard on the job every day and you will achieve success."

David attended the University of Georgia, majoring in business management with a small business specialization. Earning his Bachelor of Business Administration degree, he began working for a builder in 1992 and proceeded to incorporate his own building firm officially in 1996. Younger brother, Mark, joined David in 2004. Upon graduation from the University of Georgia with a bachelor's degree in marketing, Mark worked in the building supply business for three years. This harmonious team of brothers creates some of the Atlanta area's most beautiful suburban homes and is a member of the Greater Atlanta Home Builders Association and designated Certified Professional Home Builders. The firm was honored as the 2001 "Builder of the Week," published in the *Atlanta Journal-Constitution*.

The two talented brothers were raised in Norcross, Georgia. Together, they build primarily in gated golf communities and Atlanta area developments of Hawks Ridge, Lake Astoria and the Preserve at Fieldstone. David, the project manager in the field, oversees the building process and Mark is on site daily as lead project manager and construction supervisor. Working with noteworthy architects, the team designs and builds speculative homes that attract clients through word of mouth. Never building the same design twice, they pride themselves on building traditional and classical homes with an extraordinary amount of custom work on the interiors.

With solid work experience in every aspect of the building process, David has the knowledge and experience to see problems and correct them at all levels of the building project. Because of his eye for design and ability to create attractive curb appeal, David's houses are much sought after. David goes the extra distance to build a structurally sound house that is beautiful inside and out. Quality is never compromised.

Under the direction of David and Mark, a hand-selected team of subcontractors gives its utmost attention to detail working in tandem with homebuyers and architects. This process moves steadily and smoothly to the end result—the client's dream realized. The creative profession of building brings the firm into contact with hundreds of people, from clients to architects, tradesmen and everyone integral to the process. They love the people interaction and live amongst

LEFT:
This elegant mountain home family room has beautiful tongue-and-groove spruce lining the walls and ceilings, while antique oak planks serve as flooring. Wraparound stack stone flows into the bright kitchen with window and deck views.
Photograph by John Umberger

their clients as neighbors and friends. The highest reward is seeing clients satisfied with their homes.

Known for their trim work, original and clean-looking woodwork designs in their one-of-a-kind fireplace mantels, built-in amenities and interior column work—the firm's exquisite details have made one of their Hawks Ridge homes stand out as most impressive. The main living area's natural stone fireplace displays an intricate art piece made from an alloy metal for lightweight functionality to resemble ironwork, adding a unique dimension to the look of the room.

Their philosophy is to always do the best quality job performing to the highest standards of workmanship creating homes to be admired, appreciated and easy to live in. Southern family men and enthusiastic University of Georgia football fans, they love living, playing and working together and value being in a close-knit family business. David, Mark and Bill feel blessed by all of their success and daily apply the principles of strong family values and a persistent work ethic.

TOP RIGHT:
A massive custom bar in the finished terrace level features top-of-the-line fixtures and appliances—a perfect space for entertaining or casual relaxation with the whole family.
Photograph by John Umberger

BOTTOM RIGHT:
This spacious classical dining room with custom-made judge's paneling creates a refined, rustic feel. The fixtures, interior décor and antique random oak flooring help to make a very large, elegant room cozy and comfortable.
Photograph by John Umberger

DAVID L. FROST BUILDERS, INC.
David Frost
Mark Frost
3720 DaVinci Court, Suite 425
Norcross, GA 30092
770.729.9980
f: 770.729.9970
www.davidlfrostbuildersinc.com

MICHAEL W. GARRELL
JAMES H. KLIPPEL

Garrell Associates, Inc.

"We design the home our clients want to build, not the home we want them to build," says Michael W. Garrell. This refreshing philosophy is just one of many things that Mike has in common with James H. Klippel, his long-time partner in Garrell Associates, Inc., the award-winning Atlanta-based residential design firm.

The parallels began in Atlanta in the 1970s and have defined their phenomenally successful collaboration ever since. Though unknown to each other, they both studied architecture at Southern Technical Institute at the same time and both worked for builders during school. In the 1980s, they honed their skills working in construction-related energy initiatives as well as for local architects and builders. In 1985, their paths finally converged. Mike was a designer for a national homebuilder, while Jim was designing custom homes for an Atlanta architect. Given the parallel paths their lives had taken up until then, it was hardly

LEFT:
Timeless architecture, unique detailing and classic proportions rooted in the past evoke a sense of comfort in this French Normandy home.
Photograph by Windward Photography

surprising when they realized their shared passion for something bigger: redefining the "American home." When Mike launched the firm in 1993, he invited Jim to join him as partner.

With no pre-designed plans or a solid track record, the firm's early days were both exciting and daunting. In every design meeting with builders, they would take careful notes, and then go off to transform what they had learned into practical yet compelling residential "products." Armed with their new creations, they would go to work convincing those same builders and developers that their designs would outsell the competition. They did.

Knowing that good architectural design is the most important component of the building process, they soon saw their designs succeed in the Atlanta market. Their mastery of the design process is at the heart of their comfort level across all architectural styles. Offering both custom home designs and pre-designed home plans, their portfolio ranges from rustic mountain vacation homes to getaway beach cottages to luxury manor estates.

TOP RIGHT:
Open, airy outdoor living spaces and large windows connect nature to the indoors providing "zones of comfort" for family and friends.
Photograph by getdecorating.com

BOTTOM RIGHT:
The natural river stone fireplace with rough-hewn log mantel anchors the massing in this rustic, western-themed space on the expansive terrace level.
Photograph by getdecorating.com

FACING PAGE:
Born into the landscape this tranquil mountain home uses natural materials and massing with broad porches to create a peaceful, inviting retreat.
Photograph by getdecorating.com

Building someone's own special "castle" is an intensely personal journey, and the company has a profound respect for the process. The firm's consultants meet with each client and delve deeply into their lifestyle, needs, dreams and desires. Ideas from these brainstorming sessions evolve into home designs that are livable and functional. They then apply these and other design innovations to traditional architecture—constantly seeking new ways to move classicism in fresh and original directions. Their designs pay homage to traditional elements and rely heavily on historical precedence. They masterfully blend these classic elements into new floor plans that feature open flow and plenty of natural light.

By conservative estimate, three or more families move into a new Garrell Associates home design every day—across the country and beyond. Nearly a decade-and-a-half of designing has yielded a portfolio of over 3,000 home plans. To date, this prolific output has garnered the firm more than 200 professional awards, with numerous Street of Dreams honors in 1999, 2001, 2005 and 2006. One rustic

TOP RIGHT:
A welcoming arbor over a brick walkway leads to the stone-walled garden and charming potting shed. Shingle-style architecture defines this maritime-themed custom home.
Photograph by Kevin McManus

BOTTOM RIGHT:
Family and friends gather comfortably in the bright open kitchen and keeping room. The space opens on one side to the pool court, and the other side flows to the veranda with a summer kitchen and fireplace.
Photograph by Kevin McManus

FACING PAGE LEFT:
A beacon of spirit, this "Lightkeeper's Home" is true American architecture. All major rooms connect to the verandas for indoor and outdoor living.
Photograph by Kevin McManus

FACING PAGE RIGHT:
Seven rooms and three porches open to a red brick-paved courtyard with bridge; the luxurious soaking pool and hot tub with swim-up bar and fireplace delight the senses.
Photograph by Kevin McManus

yet elegant design for a show home in Big Canoe, Georgia, featured trusswork made from 200-year-old virgin pine logs reclaimed from a river bottom, and a kitchen with oiled, natural slate countertops. In 2006, this "Tranquility" show home earned the firm the prestigious "Best in American Living Award" (BALA) from *Professional Builder* magazine. While the considerable industry recognition has been enormously gratifying for the firm, both Mike and Jim agree that their true reward comes from knowing that thousands of people enjoy an unparalleled quality of life with their families living in the homes they have created.

The firm truly cares about each client and becomes a faithful steward of their dreams, keeping loyal clients coming back. That caring extends to their community as well. Over the years, the firm has donated design work for structures owned by the Chattahoochee Nature Center, Georgia Wildlife Federation, the Paul Anderson Youth Home and HomeAid Atlanta. For the latter's 2006 annual benefit, Project Playhouse, the firm generously designed two showcase playhouses modeled after the original Fayette County Courthouse and the St. Simons Lighthouse. This public event raised much-needed funds for Atlanta's homeless. Jim and Mike firmly believe in protecting the environment and the future of our children. The firm is always happy to donate to these worthy causes.

LEFT:
Classicism invokes America's roots in this beautiful historical reproduction of Drayton Hall near Charleston, South Carolina. The character of this antebellum Tidewater home is married to an open flowing floor plan fulfilling all the needs of family and guests.
Photograph by Garrell Associates, Inc.

FACING PAGE:
"New Urbanism"—Traditional neighborhood designs move the garage to an alley behind the home and open the classic American front porch to the sidewalk and park beyond.
Photograph by Warren Bond Photography

ABOVE LEFT:
Young and old alike can appreciate this miniature version of the renowned St. Simons Lighthouse with real lightkeeper's loft; a Project Playhouse™ award-winner.
Photograph by Garrell Associates, Inc.

ABOVE RIGHT:
The 1825 Fayette County Courthouse, the oldest courthouse in Georgia, is reproduced in child-size scale complete with clock tower, judge's bench and jail house creating a place for imaginary fun; a Project Playhouse™ award-winner.
Photograph by Garrell Associates, Inc.

FACING PAGE:
Imagine the ambience of a starry night relaxing in the hot tub with a glowing poolside fireplace; these sophisticated spa-inspired amenities pamper homeowners and their guests.
Photograph by Kevin McManus

Starting initially in the metro Atlanta area, the firm continues to expand nationally. For Mike Garrell and Jim Klippel, it is all about continuing to innovate and to grow. Every day is another opportunity to create ever better, more distinctive and more livable designs—designs that make a home a joy and a treasure. Above all, what truly drives this constantly evolving partnership is yet another thing that these two innovators have in common—a deeply shared belief that "great architecture inspires the spirit and nurtures the soul." Thousands of Garrell Associates clients would agree.

GARRELL ASSOCIATES, INC.
RESIDENTIAL DESIGN CONSULTANTS
Michael W. Garrell
James H. Klippel
790 Peachtree Industrial Boulevard,
Suite 200
Suwanee, GA 30024
770.614.3239
f: 770.614.5948
www.garrellassociates.com

ROBERT P. GOODSELL, SR.
DANIEL GOODSELL
Goodsell Associates, Inc.

Prior to the building business Bob Goodsell was serving in the U.S. Army working as a cryptographer stationed in Japan, where he co-founded an entrepreneurial venture to introduce "American-style" popcorn into the Japanese market. After 10 years, this booming business was sold to Frito-Lay, becoming the start of its snack food business.

From the popcorn business came more kernels of opportunity and Bob's newfound interest in building homes grew. He founded his predecessor company, Goodsell Construction Company, and began building custom homes in 1969 as principal contractors in north metro Atlanta. From historic Buckhead to Vinings, North Fulton to Sandy Springs, this deeply rooted urban Atlanta building business has branched out into suburbia, now building 80 percent new custom homes and some historic renovations.

LEFT:
The Griffin home of Atlanta's famed Buckhead exemplifies a villa residence with classical columns, natural slate roof, Old World stucco exterior and hand-laid stonework—built to blend seamlessly into the wooded landscape. Architecture by Jack Gimson.
Photograph by James Lockhart

Keeping a low profile and very high standards is the 35-year-long philosophy of Goodsell Associates. Joined by nephew Danny Goodsell in 1980, this dynamic pair has been constructing luxury custom residences and developing property in the prime northwest Atlanta area. With an affinity for building classic and traditional homes and architectural designs based on historical precedence, the firm works with Atlanta's preeminent architects. In this elite $1.5 million-plus custom home category, Goodsell Associates exclusively custom-builds four homes annually with a handful of renovations sprinkled in for good measure.

Bob's brother Dick was a successful developer who influenced him to enter the development business, as his model of quality was an inspiration. Bob wanted to avoid building competing architectural statements so he began developing residential communities partnering with Joel Griffin of The Griffin Company to maintain historical accuracy creating beautiful traditional neighborhoods. Bob is an active member and past director of local, state and national boards including the Greater Atlanta Home Builders Association, Home Builders Association of Georgia and National Association of Home Builders. In 2006, the firm was awarded the "Best Single Family Home—$2,500,000 and Above" from the Greater Atlanta

LEFT:
The Mills home in historic Buckhead evokes a welcoming Southern hospitality. Cedar shake shingles, multiple dormers, shuttered windows and stone chimney are befitting of the established neighborhood. Residential design by William T. Baker.
Photograph by James Lockhart

FACING PAGE TOP:
The Baker home in the renowned community of Sandy Springs is an architecturally unpretentious style featuring an elaborate stonework exterior, inviting covered front porch and complex wood-shingled roofline. Architecture by Jack Gimson.
Photograph by James Lockhart

FACING PAGE BOTTOM LEFT:
The Baker home's country-inspired sitting room is elegance personified with custom antiqued woodwork, graceful built-in cabinetry and carved stone mantelpiece. Twelve-foot ceilings have meticulous crown mouldings and generous windows invite rays of Georgia sunlight.
Photograph by James Lockhart

FACING PAGE BOTTOM RIGHT:
Details abound in the grand hall of the Masco home in Atlanta—impressive 30-foot ceilings and classic Palladian windows create spaciousness. Refined detailing provides the perfect backdrop for art masterpieces and classical mural designs.
Photograph courtesy of Goodsell Associates

Home Builders Association making it the proud recipient of a total of four awards for high-end luxury home-building, including the national "Grand Award" for homes over 4,000 square feet. Their award-winning, quality residences have been featured in *Southern Living*, *Metropolitan Homes*, *Southern Homes*, *Better Homes and Gardens*, *Southeastern Home*, *Builder Magazine*, *Atlanta Homes & Lifestyles*, *Atlanta Home Book*, *Atlanta Source Guild*, *Home Magazine*, *Professional Builder* and the *Atlanta Journal-Constitution*.

What makes this professional builder different is its special treatment of each client as a separate business, so as a home is built it has an independent accounting system in place. This provides comfort to the client; close-cost controls, monthly reports and careful monitoring make the building process more palatable and enjoyable overall. Very selective about their subcontractors and the clients with whom they work, Bob and Danny Goodsell foster good friendships, having fun with a sense of humor, guaranteeing a pleasant process and mutual success at the end of the day.

The name of the game for this professional firm is having a "family" of the best subcontractors—most of whom have been loyal for more than 20 years to maintain quality construction standards, providing exceptional detail work. The traditional American classic home is the Goodsell trademark and the ever-expanding Atlanta area allows them the freedom to build stately, architecturally correct homes for the most gracious Southern lifestyle.

GOODSELL ASSOCIATES, INC.
Robert P. Goodsell Sr.
Daniel Goodsell
PO Box 720513
Atlanta, GA 30358
404.352.9660
f: 404.352.9663
www.goodsellassociates.com

DAVID GRACE
LAMAR WAKEFIELD
JOHN B. BEASLEY JR.
MATT MASTIN

A Classical Studio

ABOVE:
Pristine fluted Ionic columns support the stately front entrance.
Photograph by Walter Elliott

FACING PAGE:
This gracious red brick Colonial Revival residence is located in a renowned, historic Atlanta neighborhood.
Photograph by Walter Elliott

David Grace, president of A Classical Studio, is a residential designer with a degree in architecture from Southern Polytechnic State University. Early in his career, David began taking classes with the Institute of Classical Architecture in New York, which influenced him so greatly that it changed the direction of his career path. After completing his certificate in classical architecture, David became an active member of the organization. Endeavoring to bring classical education to architects throughout the Southeast, David helped start the first local chapter of the Institute of Classical Architecture. The philosophy of A Classical Studio reflects the values of timeless design, practicing classical and traditional architecture. A search for meaning in architecture led David to his belief in the expressive nature of the classical vocabulary and the beauty of traditional forms. The ideals of architectural design, "Firmness, Commodity and Delight," first written around 25 B.C. by the Roman architect Vitruvius, guide the philosophy of A Classical Studio in its practice today.

While A Classical Studio was founded in 2003, the firm's partners, David Grace, R. Lamar Wakefield, AIA, John B. Beasley Jr., AIA, and John Mathew Mastin, AIA, have more than 50 years of collective, award-winning architectural experience. David shares his zeal for classical and traditional architecture with all the members of the Studio, creating a wonderful synergy when working on each custom home. Each project begins with a precedent study to ensure that the new design will be correct in style, indigenous to its location and deeply rooted in the classical tradition. The work of A Classical Studio ensures an architectural integrity based on the local vernacular paired with modern amenities. These new houses are pleasing to the eye as well as convenient for daily life in the 21st century.

The Studio has designed houses for discerning Georgia clients who want classically inspired homes on scenic Lake Lanier and Lake Burton as well as turn-of-the-century historic neighborhoods of Atlanta. Homes by A Classical Studio also grace the marshlands of South Carolina low country, the sunny beach communities of Florida's panhandle and acreage in St. Thomas, U.S. Virgin Islands. In Pine Mountain, the progressive firm designed tree houses that whimsically float above the forest floor while applying an ecological, Green approach to the land below. Whether it is the client's primary custom residence or a second-home retreat, A Classical Studio stays true to the design principles of classical architecture.

LEFT:
This rustic and welcoming vernacular mountain cabin is set amidst fall foliage in scenic Cashiers, North Carolina.
Photograph by Walter Elliott

FACING PAGE:
A gable and hexagon tower grace this Shingle-style beach cottage.
Photograph by David Grace

The design architects hand-draw every home design and translate it into a working model using CAD technology for accuracy in the field. David considers the firm to be creators of "ideal lifestyles" because they design custom homes and work to fulfill the dreams and desires of each client by weaving together exterior and interior aesthetics with circulation patterns and furniture layouts. A Classical Studio applies a perfectionist mindset to the selection of colors, finishes, patterns and textures to achieve impeccable interior design. This highly sophisticated specialty of designing custom luxury residential homes with utmost attention to detail is the Studio's signature.

Extraordinarily dedicated to the client relationship, the firm exhibits a contagious enthusiasm throughout every project. David Grace had a boyhood enthusiasm for building tree houses and three dimensional scale models of towns, and today it is this passionate expression of creative talent that fuels the acclaimed studio to design some of the most beautiful, traditional homes throughout Georgia and the Southeast.

A CLASSICAL STUDIO

David W. Grace, ICA/CA
Lamar Wakefield, AIA
John B. Beasley Jr., AIA
Matt Mastin, AIA
5155 Peachtree Parkway, Suite 300
Norcross, GA 30092
770.248.2800
f: 770.248.2801
www.aclassicalstudio.com

ABOVE:
Custom leaded-glass china cabinet doors and an arched transom inform this Federal-style formal dining room.
Photograph by Fred Gerlich

FACING PAGE:
The front elevation of a beach house faces a pedestrian boardwalk. The deep front porches become outdoor living rooms with beach views—lookout a tower rises above.
Photograph by Abby Caroline Mims

WILLIAM H. HARRISON
GREGORY L. PALMER
ANTHONY P. SPANN
Harrison Design Associates

Sketching with pencil at every opportunity, William (Bill) H. Harrison, AIA, fell in love with art and architecture at the tender age of 12. An ambitious young man during his high school years, Bill gleaned his basic training in the field of architecture while apprenticing for a Macon architectural firm under the tutelage of Henry Dixon. It was this positive, early work experience that inspired him to turn a boyhood dream into reality.

Earning his degree in architecture from Georgia Institute of Technology, Bill subsequently opened his first design-build company in Atlanta, Georgia, in 1978. After 13 years of practicing the art of home designing and building, he founded his own architectural firm, Harrison Design Associates of Atlanta, in 1991.

LEFT:
In order to maximize the beauty of the site, the design incorporates large windows that bring in abundant light, as well as a series of terraces and loggias to encourage a blend of indoor and outdoor living. The natural surroundings also provided inspiration for the material and color selections. The retaining walls and portions of the home's façade are made of site-quarried sandstone.
Photograph by Jim Bartsch

Today, with a hand-picked design team of more than 80 architects and designers, the company has strategically attracted the finest talent from the United States and many foreign countries who are prepared to plan, design and build fine residences and commercial projects for people throughout the state of Georgia. Harrison Design Associates has offices in Atlanta and St. Simons Island, Georgia, as well as Santa Barbara and Beverly Hills, California. Principal and veteran architect, Greg Palmer, AIA, is a managing partner for the East Coast and Tony Spann, AIA, is the West Coast managing partner. This well-built, innovative firm composed of individual operational studios works on architectural design projects throughout the contiguous United States and in several countries around the world.

The firm refers to its structure as a "we" team, knowing it takes quality individuals working in unison together to run a successful organization. Above and beyond the architectural team and its residential and commercial projects are the many community organizations that the firm is dedicated to serving in the Atlanta area. Giving back to the community is of utmost importance. From historical preservation of buildings and support for botanical gardens, to exacting renovation, beautiful, integrative additions and new structures, Harrison Design Associates is adding to the social and cultural tapestry of Georgia, enriching people living in or near its award-winning designs.

Harrison Design Associates has the rare luxury of drawing on the large firm's collective expertise and vast resources, incorporating quality construction methodology, historic knowledge and an affinity for genuine materials with Old World craftsmanship, utilizing contemporary artisans to bring a dream home to life. Whether the firm is designing a 1,200-square-foot space, a sprawling 30,000-square-foot mansion or an 800-square-foot porch addition, the commitment to excellence is consistent.

LEFT:
Warm materials of wood, stucco and stone, unique details such as the timber ceiling and carved beams and soft fabric panels create a terrace as luxurious and dreamy as the view it offers.
Photograph by Jim Bartsch

FACING PAGE:
This stately Georgian estate rendered in brick and limestone is adorned with copper accents such as conductor heads, downspouts and lanterns. The symmetrical qualities of this style afford an overall balance and harmony to the design, while the pedimented entry with Palladian window above give distinct character and focus to the center of the façade.
Photograph by John Umberger

Designing private ecclesiastic structures, special commercial projects and private residences for prominent executives, professional athletes, entertainment moguls and real estate developers, the renowned team fulfills the dream of each and every client. It is a very personal experience and an honor to help each client plan, design and create a home to reflect their given lifestyle within the context of community. Moreover, quality architectural designs add to the social fabric of a community and offer something lasting for people to appreciate, giving them enjoyment, enlightenment and a sense of well-being and security.

The founder's greatest influence is the work of early 15th-century Italian classical architect Andrea Palladio. Early in his career, Bill traveled to Italy to study Palladio's acclaimed Renaissance architecture, inspiring him to make continuing education a part of his firm's philosophy. The firm stresses the importance of knowing Greek and Roman geometry and proportion as well as understanding classical roots so one can be "true" to any style of architecture. Then, and only then, can an architect apply it to modern classical design and build structures with good bones. Harrison Design Associates has taken traditional, classical architecture into the 21st century by applying the rules, foundation and roots to current, everyday solutions. They use a modern approach to architecture that is grounded in the past. The essence of their philosophy is simply this: "Architecture is not about copying the past. It's about taking the best from both past and present, and combining the two into the best possible creation."

RIGHT:
A white bronze backsplash is the perfect backdrop for the natural stone surround of the hood and range. Rustic honey-toned wood and painted cabinets serve to lighten the space. The large central island allows for easy food preparation and entertaining while enjoying the family's prized jukebox.
Photograph by John Umberger

FACING PAGE LEFT:
Asymmetrical layering of the entrance and turret create dynamic balance in a design connecting Arts-and-Crafts with Queen Anne style. An assortment of roof, porch and window designs convey informality and capricious charm at every angle.
Photograph by Gil Stose

FACING PAGE RIGHT:
Natural materials such as the antler chandelier, rustic wood ceiling and stone fireplace support the amazing lake and mountain views in this family room.
Photograph by John Umberger

Understanding that traveling to see original work in natural settings inspires more authentically than anything from books or photographs, their leadership is committed to providing architectural tour experiences for professional staff prior to beginning important projects. As a result, the architect team takes into careful consideration the environment and site selection, contextually integrating the architectural design.

One such project in Dahlonega, Georgia, is about combining commercial work with residential work to create a living vineyard community. The design includes a 400-acre vineyard with wine-tasting rooms, upscale restaurants, grand estate homes on the river and country villas that were inspired by visiting existing Italian vineyards. The architectural team is involved in planning, building and creating all of the elements to birth a vineyard village that is an integral part of the landscape. This development design directly relates to an authentic vineyard community experience and the "draw from the true source" philosophy is the basis for this exceptional planned community project.

Singlepointedly, the goal of each project is to interpret the client's vision yet surpass what people can imagine in their own minds. Creating the ultimate home and designing beyond expectations means working more efficiently, using imagination, intelligence and analytical thinking.

TOP RIGHT:
Gentle breaks in massing and the use of distinct design elements artfully obscure the scale of this expansive home. Indigenous materials unite this European manor home with the surrounding grounds, creating a haven of unassuming grace.
Photograph by John Umberger

BOTTOM RIGHT:
The arrangement of this paneled dining room provides maximum access and flexibility for entertaining. Located adjacent to the kitchen and living room, the dining room is the central gathering location in the home. Two smaller dining tables easily reconfigure to accommodate intimate or large gatherings.
Photograph by Jonathan Harper

FACING PAGE:
Classical detailing, proportion and scale were guiding factors in the design of this historically based Georgian-style home. Symmetrical loggias, flanking a series of French doors with transoms above, allow effortless flow between the home and the pool and gardens beyond.
Photograph by John Umberger

TOP:
The front façade of this Beaux-Arts estate features 10 solid-shaft Indiana limestone columns, along with six pilasters, to support the ornately carved pediment and cornice of the covered front porch.
Photograph by John Umberger

FACING PAGE:
Solid Rouge de Roi columns with gilded Ionic capitals encircle the home's entry vestibule. From the entry, the view into the dining room features the room's antique Italian fireplace's surround and chandelier, gilded columns and shallow domed ceiling.
Photograph by John Umberger

Altogether, it is an exhilarating experience to use knowledge and ability, coupled with problem-solving skills and creativity, to develop an original design. It is this passionate spirit that lives and breathes in the firm every day.

The diverse architectural team can design and build homes in a variety of styles borrowing from the classical past with an eye to the future, all the while building a reputation clients appreciate. This dynamic group strives together to deliver the highest quality in all that they do and has the added benefit of drawing upon the partners and senior architects for their valuable expertise. Having a unique organizational structure, the architects and designers literally run their individual studios and serve clients directly under the umbrella of the firm allowing them to truly "own" each project from start to finish. In fact, the highest compliment has been from real estate professionals who affirm that the company has "raised the bar" for everyone working in the architecture and design industry. For more than 15 years, it is this professional respect and trust factor that wins Harrison Design Associates a loyal following.

What the firm finds best about designing in the Atlanta area is the growing nature of this landmark city rich in history, traditional identity and Southern roots. The principals' vision to always maintain true historic quality, yet transcend tradition by presenting architectural designs in new ways is now a recognized model in the modern world of architecture.

Harrison Design Associates
William H. Harrison, AIA
Gregory L. Palmer, AIA
Anthony P. Spann, AIA
3198 Cains Hill Place, Suite 200
Atlanta, GA 30305
866.688.3988
404.365.7760
www.harrisondesignassociates.com

KAREN ELLIS HINDEN
Designs For Living

K aren Ellis Hinden is the president, founder and principal residential designer of Designs For Living. With an entrepreneurial spirit, Karen is a high-energy individual whose artistic talent and passion for architecture has led her to design some of metro Atlanta's most beautiful custom and speculative homes.

Beginning as an imaginative child artist and pianist, she graduated from Oral Roberts University with a Bachelor of Arts degree in piano and minor in art. After working as a visual merchandising manager in the retail environment, Karen continued her education at Horry Georgetown Technical College, earning a drafting diploma with architectural emphasis. In 1986 she relocated to Atlanta and gained employment with a prominent residential design firm as an architectural draftsperson. It was here that she discovered her true passion. Inspired to design, in 1988 Karen established Designs For Living and began to do freelance designs of speculative homes for builders. Her designs quickly gained attention and she has been designing homes of excellence, custom and speculative, for 18 years.

ABOVE:
Impressive segmental arches, stucco and natural stone details with wrought-iron balconies create elegance and uniqueness in this French-inspired home.
Photograph by Jason Perkins Designs

FACING PAGE:
Castello Di Amici or "Castle of Friends" stands majestic upon this corner lot. An angled grand entrance enables the front elevation to be continuous around the corner with street exposure on three sides.
Photograph by Jason Perkins Designs

The ability to truly listen to the client's needs and desires has set her apart from other designers. She has the innate intuition to comprehend each client's needs and guides them through a design process that results in their envisioned dream home. Karen's tenacious personality, creative talent and careful attention to detail enable her to design all styles of architecture. From the graceful lines of classical design to the freer, relaxed beach cottage, she has done them all with an ever-remarkable gift for excellence in floor plan and elevation design.

The interior space of all of her plans is well thought out, combining creativity with functionality, always creating an exciting interior perfect for families to move freely within the home. She enjoys the challenge of angles in a floor plan, creating an unexpected interior sometimes combined with a classical façade. Her husband and two daughters graciously accept her time away from home working as a creative businesswoman, which has given her personal experience to genuinely understand the true needs of a modern, growing family.

Creating custom homes with a certain "wow" factor has become her signature. From one-bedroom guest retreats to spacious custom homes with spectacular lake views, Karen believes they are all "dream homes" to someone, regardless of size. She designs the architectural bones working hand-in-hand with the builder and finishes with the interior designer to create award-winning residences. Her work has been published in *Better Homes and Gardens* magazine and *The Builder's Link*, a local builder magazine. She designed the Roswell Women's Club Decorator's Show Home 1997 and her designs have also received Gold and Silver OBIE awards from the Greater Atlanta Home Builders Association.

Karen's attitude of gratitude for every client is evident upon introduction and her designer-client relationships are professional with one-on-one personalized attention. Patient throughout the creative process, working closely with the client, builder and interior designer, she creates remarkable one-of-a-kind homes of superior design. Karen believes that with great blessing comes great responsibility and the ultimate award she receives is a satisfied client.

DESIGNS FOR LIVING

Karen Ellis Hinden

770 Old Roswell Place, Suite 400C

Roswell, GA 30076

678.277.8658

f: 770.592.7699

www.designsforlivingga.com

ABOVE:
Castello Di Amici's rear elevation features large expanses of glass and multiple-covered verandas. Three master suites and three guest suites along with numerous living areas all enjoy the view of the lake beyond.
Photograph by Jason Perkins Designs

FACING PAGE TOP:
The combination of a stone-and-brick exterior, along with graceful curves and arches, gives this Country French residence a storybook charm that is warm and welcoming at dusk or dawn.
Photograph by Jason Perkins Designs

FACING PAGE BOTTOM:
A challenging narrow lot led to a courtyard front entry; gothic arches and high-pitched gables provide character and appeal. Although this speculative home appears small, it actually boasts 8,000 square feet.
Photograph by Jason Perkins Designs

HISTORICAL CONCEPTS
Architects, Planners & Place-Makers

With a diverse body of work spanning a quarter of a century, Historical Concepts embraces a design philosophy rooted in the time-honored practices of traditional architecture and planning. Now a multidisciplinary partnership offering residential architecture, commercial architecture and land planning services, Historical Concepts was founded in 1982 by James L. Strickland, who continues to lead the firm as its president and senior principal.

As its name suggests, Historical Concepts remains true to America's architectural heritage, focusing on creating homes, streets and communities that are steeped in tradition. Whether they have been commissioned to design a small cottage, an urban townhouse or a sprawling plantation, the design teams at Historical Concepts start each project by studying the unique features of the site, as well as the local architectural precedent, to provide the client with an authentically styled home that respects and complements its surroundings. By continually weaving the exterior and interior of each home until all elements work in concert, the firm crafts timeless façades

ABOVE LEFT:
Well composed details, such as furniture-like vanities with honed marble tops, antique lighting, pilastered trim and wide-plank antique pine flooring with a wax finish, evoke the feeling of a true historic home.
Photograph by Richard Leo Johnson/Atlantic Archives

ABOVE RIGHT:
Interior elements, such as this substantial Greek Revival door casing and operable transom, contribute to the authenticity of design through period-appropriate detailing.
Photograph by Richard Leo Johnson/Atlantic Archives

that are pleasing from every vantage point and floor plans that reflect the client's unique lifestyle.

A successful architectural business that has grown steadily mainly by word-of-mouth referrals, the firm has evolved into a creative team of more than 30 design professionals all sharing a passion for the timeless "sense of place" found in historic cities and towns. Led by Jim Strickland and partners Todd Strickland, Terry Pylant, Aaron Daily and Andrew Cogar, the team is hand-picked from the nation's top traditional architecture programs to ensure that the firm's culture of excellence will endure. Together, the firm's ultimate vision is to create new homes, neighborhoods and communities of equal quality, charm and value that will be a legacy for future generations.

With an imaginative design approach and a keen sensitivity to the client's needs and desires, Historical Concepts' homes exude a rich, regional flavor and span a full spectrum of architectural styles and typologies. Having designed some of the most remarkable private residences from New York to Florida, the firm's work has been featured in many national publications and has garnered numerous design awards.

A native of Atlanta, Jim Strickland was greatly influenced by the works of Neel Reid, Edward Vason Jones and Philip Shutze. He found early inspiration not just in Atlanta's gracious mansions, but in the quaint streets of small towns throughout the Southeast. Today, Strickland is surrounded by an accomplished team that shares his exuberant enthusiasm for turn-of-the-century architecture. By following timeless design principles and utilizing the synergy of an experienced and energetic team, Historical Concepts is known for creating new homes and communities that appear as if they have been an authentic part of the landscape for generations.

HISTORICAL CONCEPTS
ARCHITECTS, PLANNERS & PLACE-MAKERS
430 Prime Point, Suite 103
Peachtree City, GA 30269
770.487.8041
f: 770.487.5418
www.historicalconcepts.com

ABOVE:
Rising above the marshes of the North Newport River near Savannah, this Greek Revival antebellum plantation home pays homage to Old World architecture and craftsmanship.
Photograph by Chip Cooper

M. DEANE JOHNSON
Johnson, Williams & Harris, LLC

For nearly 100 years, the family of Deane Johnson has been building beautiful residences throughout Atlanta. One could say that architecture and real estate has been its lifelong passion.

In 1908, Deane's great-grandfather, John Lampkin Harper, entered the real estate firm of Sturgeon Realty Company and in 1911, he founded Harper Realty Company; John's wife Adelle founded Harper's Flowers on the corner of West Peachtree Street and 14th, employing two of her sons, Doyal Alexander and architect William Bartlett. Before going to work at the flower shop, William designed many homes in Buckhead for the famed architectural firm Cooper and Cooper. The next generation continued the businesses with Adelle's daughter, Auverne Harper Brady, operating Harper's Flowers for 50 years—she celebrated her 98th birthday in December 2006. John Lampkin Harper Jr. began working for the established realty firm and

the Harper family eventually sold its private residence on West Paces Ferry to the Atlanta Historical Society where the Atlanta History Center now graces the original home site—they since have sold their florist business property on West Peachtree and the IBM building now stands in its place. Amazingly, both sides of Deane's family were in the real estate world and his paternal grandmother, Rebecca Morris Johnson, was a successful broker with Pete Klein Realty, Brannan & Schmitz Realty and Harry Norman Realtors.

Prior to joining the family business himself, Deane completed coursework in building science at Auburn University, earned a bachelor's degree in business and behavior from Oglethorpe University and a master's degree in divinity from New Orleans Seminary. Deane learned the essentials of the custom homebuilding business for 12 years from his father at the Bob Johnson Development Company. Deane's father, Robert (Bob) Morris Johnson, founded R.M. Johnson Builders, Inc. in 1956, influencing the look of Atlanta architecture in the '50s and '60s from the trend of Ranch-style houses to the more traditional architecture we associate with present-day Atlanta. His visionary father also pioneered the development of North Harbor and Breakwater communities along the banks of the Chattahoochee River.

Growing up in an aesthetically rich environment, Deane learned the importance of colors, texture and creativity in design. Deane's thorough study of old Atlanta has provided the contextual foundation for his firm to recreate traditional, historic residences using modern building technologies and products. Since incorporating in 1984, Deane Johnson and company have taken the building business to a new level in Atlanta. They lovingly restored one of the

LEFT:
The foyer stays true to its fascination with the Regency details of geometric shapes and classical proportions.
Photograph by Pam Smart

FACING PAGE:
The terrace overlooks 18 acres of pristine pasture and is supported by 4,000-pound computer-lathed, solid limestone Doric columns with carved matching limestone balustrade.
Photograph by Pam Smart

most famous Georgian homes in the area, which suffered severe fire damage in 2000. Their work was acknowledged and the firm received The Georgia Trust 2003 Preservation Award for Excellence in Rehabilitation. This estate is the most photographed home in Atlanta, and as legend has it, actors Clark Gable and Vivien Leigh held a lavish party for the premiere of the film classic "Gone With the Wind" at this very residence. The gracious historical home was featured in the March-April 2007 issue of *Veranda* magazine.

Recently, Deane's firm built out the North Penthouse tower at 2500 Peachtree Road to become one client's urban "city" home for elegant entertaining. The interior look was created by a well-known Parisian designer. This home boasts the most expensive square footage of any residence in the city of Atlanta. Even the smallest details are masterfully executed, from the salon's floors with diamond-patterned, unglazed Negev limestone and waxed antique wood to the master bathroom, complete with book-matched honey-onyx and colored glass tile, oversized onyx-clad soaking Bain massage bathtub and 14-carat gold fixtures. The spectacular and unique penthouse has become a "cover story," appearing in the Winter 2007 issue of the *Atlanta Registry* magazine.

Another impressive Deane Johnson Atlanta development is West Paces Park, a private gated community near the landmark Governor's Mansion. West Paces Park is a 12-plus-acre community built to feel as though you were driving into a neighborhood built in the 1920s and 1930s. Deane commissioned Bill Harrison & Associates, William T. Baker, Spitzmiller & Norris and John Oetgen & Associates to recreate the look and feel of old Buckhead.

The most expensive renovation in the city is also attributed to Johnson & Williams, LLC. A two-year renovation on West Conway took the residence from 14,000 to 25,000 square feet. The home was originally built by Johnson & Williams, LLC for Neiman Marcus and *Southern Accents* magazine as the original Holiday House to benefit AID Atlanta. *Southern Accents* magazine featured this custom residence as the front cover photograph for the December 1998 issue, and again in January 2007 after its renovation. This home boasts the most elaborate spaces found in the Southeastern United States, from barreled tongue-in-groove pecky cypress ceilings in the living area to custom-designed formal mouldings, hand-carved Corinthian columns, imported French and Mediterranean limestone floors and twin 18th-century Italian lead crystal chandeliers.

Deane's relationship with these clients extends far beyond a standard business relationship. In 2002, Deane was invited to host his wedding ceremony and reception in the front yard of the West Conway residence, and today their families are still close. Deane also has friendships with many of his contractors, especially Don Cloud, who was Deane's father's electrician in 1968 before he left to serve our country in Vietnam—Don is still on the job everyday and is one of Deane's dearest friends.

TOP LEFT:
With panoramic city views, this hand-milled, antique heart pine kitchen is wrapped with 100-year-old heart pine beams, ceilings and ship-lapped walls.
Photograph by Pam Smart

BOTTOM LEFT:
Cypress is the beautiful wood of choice for this custom gourmet kitchen featuring built-in custom cabinetry and a massive butcher block island.
Photograph by Pam Smart

FACING PAGE LEFT:
The pecky cypress barrel-vaulted ceiling warms this authentic Regency family space. Custom metal doors crafted in England flank the high-tech entertainment center; an automated wood panel raises and lowers at the push of a button to reveal the flat-screen television.
Photograph by Pam Smart

FACING PAGE RIGHT:
The Parisian interior designer's sophisticated touch is evident in the grand salon of this elegant penthouse—an urban residential project boasting the most expensive cost-per-square-foot in the Southeast.
Photograph by Pam Smart

ABOVE:
This romantic French Normandy country manor with its pleasing combination of tumbled limestone, painted clinkered brick and authentic Spanish slate roof is the personal home of the featured builder. In the fall of 2006, this home was featured as the front cover of "The Atlanta Collection."
Photograph by Johnson & Williams, LLC

FACING PAGE:
In keeping with the classical homes of old Atlanta, this glorious master bath is enveloped by a series of intersecting groin vaults, a signature of the refined details one can expect in a Deane Johnson home.
Photograph by Vawter Vision at Jenny Pruitt & Associates

Deane has recently partnered with Ed Grenvicz, Jim Elliot, Joel Griffin, Richard Williams and Richard Harris. Following his father's dream, Deane has expanded his career into residential land development, partnering with his younger brother, Cyrus Johnson, and Jody Pierce. This relationship has led to a building partnership with Sonny and Bray Devours. Deane relates: "Brayson Homes builds a superior product that I feel represents the quality on which I would base my own reputation."

Deane sees the building business as an opportunity to make a difference in the community. In addition to the Holiday House for AID Atlanta, the Regent Park House at West Paces Park, the Georgian House and the Art Atlanta 2005 Art House were sold to raise funds benefiting the American Diabetes Association, Georgia Transplant Foundation, Heartline Ministries and Child Kind, to name a few.

As the love of building and architecture has been handed down to him, Deane is creating a living legacy for his children and generations to come. Deane believes that his role as builder can be likened to the director of an orchestra conducting a highly talented group of accomplished artists, all working in concert together to create lasting historical architecture.

JOHNSON, WILLIAMS & HARRIS, LLC
M. Deane Johnson
8097 Roswell Road
Building F, Suite 100
Atlanta, GA 30350
770.399.6869
f: 770.399.5870
www.jw-h.com

PATRICK R. KIRKLAND
LAURA M. POTTS
KARIN K. GREEN
Kirkland + Associates Architects, PC

The summer of 1983 was significant for Patrick Kirkland, AIA. This was the year he co-founded his first architectural firm, but it was in April of 1993 when Pat bought the small commercial business, taking it to the next level with talented architects Laura M. Potts, AIA, and Karin K. Green, AIA. To diversify its already successful practice, the team decided to focus on the luxury custom-residential design market for clients that included both long-time residents and corporate professionals transferring to the fast-growing Atlanta area.

With Pat at the helm, the team of three architects combined creative forces to design multimillion-dollar private residences throughout Atlanta. The majority of their custom work is in exclusive suburban developments, second homes in Florida's Rosemary Beach, Georgia's scenic North Mountains and various locales throughout the Southeast. The architect partners work together with adept project managers as well as staff intern architects who transform their original hand-drawn designs into final construction documents.

Both Atlanta natives, Pat studied architecture at Southern Tech and Laura received her architectural degree from Georgia Tech. Karin also earned her bachelor's degree at Southern Tech and together the firm has been winning awards for its incomparable designs. Receiving first-place OBIE Awards from the Greater Atlanta Home Builders Association and notable national awards, their reputation stands on their collective design experience. Designing more than 80 percent custom residential work as well as commercial projects including hotels, clubhouses and wellness centers associated with residential communities, the team is licensed and NCARB certified in several states throughout the Southeast. Their extraordinary homes have been featured in *Atlanta Homes & Lifestyles* magazine and showcased in the Sugarloaf Country Club Holiday Tour of Homes.

LEFT:
This custom English Manor home was designed to fit in seamlessly within its beautiful natural setting; appropriate professional landscaping adds to the effect.
Photograph by Paul Dingman

FACING PAGE:
An inviting outdoor living room provides a welcome retreat in this custom residence.
Photograph by Paul Dingman

Kirkland + Associates Architects masterfully designs large-scale custom homes and has an impressive 20,000-square-foot English country manor to its credit. The firm was commissioned to design a custom residence reminiscent of The Grove Park Inn in Asheville, North Carolina. The client requested lodge-like features including an oversized stone fireplace and generous exterior porches overlooking the 18th green and fairway and beautiful private lake. This unique home is poised on 2.8 acres in a gated golf course community and the team saw the woodlands, lake and golf course setting as an architectural opportunity to integrate the home brilliantly into the landscape. In keeping with their core philosophy to design homes in proportion to a rolling site and with regard to its environment, they designed an elevated platform for the Bell South Classic with room to ensure a 270-degree view of the open fairway. A well-sited home designed respectfully in relationship with the land is a Kirkland + Associates Architects hallmark.

The firm specializes in English manor homes as well as architectural styles that encompass the same qualities of being less formal with a distinctively traditional feel. Atlanta clients prefer various forms of traditional architecture and the firm designs beautiful Country French and Tuscany-inspired homes that are representative of European architecture. Partner Laura M. Potts travels abroad for research to inspire the designs with detailed authenticity. Elegant and classic, Kirkland + Associates Architects' custom residences are designed to stand the test of time for generations to come.

TOP RIGHT:
The courtyards and porches of this English manor provide outdoor living areas that extend the indoor experience to the rear grounds.
Photograph by Paul Dingman

BOTTOM RIGHT:
Broad steps lead to the hand-carved limestone formal entry of this English manor.
Photograph by Paul Dingman

FACING PAGE:
The use of limestone and slate give this English Manor an elegant sense of history.
Photograph by Paul Dingman

Pat Kirkland is an innovator in the residential architecture field and formed a "Design Guild" for Atlanta developers. He hand-selected architects and residential designers to establish the initial look and feel for a new community, designating a review architect to guide developers in building speculative and custom homes that meet the highest design standards.

Kirkland + Associates Architects interviews each client in-depth to determine their family lifestyle, desires and dreams. Understanding the client's perspective thoroughly, Pat and his team offer design solutions and expertise that truly relates to their unique goals. Listening intently to their client's vision of the perfect home before the creative process ever begins allows the design to unfold strategically. The fresh challenge of creating an aesthetic design and developing an architectural solution inspires the team on a daily basis.

LEFT:
A stone walk leads to this French Chateau-inspired design with aged stucco and iron brackets.
Photograph by Paul Dingman

FACING PAGE:
A freestanding soaking tub is the highlight of this master bathroom.
Photograph by Bob Thein

Kirkland + Associates Architects takes great pride in knowing that its clientele come strictly through its design reputation and referrals from other satisfied clients. With their expertise and communication skills they enlighten clients to make appropriate design decisions every step of the way to a beautiful new home. It is this mutual trust factor that is the essence of their success.

KIRKLAND + ASSOCIATES ARCHITECTS, PC
Patrick R. Kirkland, AIA
Laura M. Potts, AIA
Karin K. Green, AIA
4488 North Shallowford Road, Suite 110
Atlanta, GA 30338
770.396.9966
f: 770.396.9676
www.kirklandarchitects.com

GEORGE KRITKO
VICKI KRITKO
Country Classic Builders, Inc.

The spirit of excellence and creativity is the soul of George and Vicki Kritko's custom homebuilding company. They are a match made in both marriage and business. It all started in 1986 when the newlyweds built their very first home for themselves. They received an offer on their home while living there and an idea was born.

For the last 20 years their love for each other has grown as did their love of homebuilding. They continued on a journey of building and selling that eventually led to the founding of Country Classic Builders. This husband-and-wife team exclusively builds customized residences for its Georgia clientele, tapping into its joint "unlimited creativity." George directs the big-picture, design-build process while Vicki takes clients through the materials, decorating and amenities selection, resulting in an impeccably crafted home. Their philosophy is to start and finish a home with the same enthusiasm so the end result exceeds the client's expectations and meets their high standards of excellence. As a result, their beautifully built residences have been featured in *Today's Custom Homes* magazine.

ABOVE:
The master bathroom exudes a luxury spa feel with chiseled travertine throughout, barrel-vaulted ceilings and walk-around shower creating a relaxed atmosphere. A plasma television in custom cabinetry offers entertainment pleasure. Interior design by Lynn Mock of Monet Gardens.
Photograph by John Umberger

FACING PAGE:
This mountain estate-inspired custom residence boasts an exterior of cedar shake shingle and Tennessee fieldstone reminiscent of a rustic lodge, yet is situated in a Columbus golf course community.
Photograph by John Umberger

The couple enjoys helping clients express themselves through their chosen style of architecture and interprets their vision as an extension of family. The art of homebuilding provides unlimited possibilities to the Kritko team, so they begin the process meeting with each client, sketching concepts and developing a plan to make it happen. Styles range from Mediterranean to upscale Craftsman and their research begins the moment they receive their client's input. Whether they travel to Tuscany for inspiration or visit national home shows to see innovative building trends at the "Street of Dreams" showcases, their solutions are beautiful and functional to fit the lifestyles of suburban families.

Homebuyers are seeking well-appointed gourmet kitchens because they have become the central focus of most American homes. This is where Vicki makes sure her clients always experience an inviting warmth in the room by using natural stone fireplaces, granite countertops and well-turned cabinetry to create the family's gathering place. The artisans and craftsmen they employ are experts in the business and the finished quality speaks for itself. Using natural materials in an artful way makes the details of every Country Classic Builders home something to admire.

Uncommon built-in features add a sense of personalization to a custom home and these special "extras" make all the difference. One carriage house project featured recycled oak barrels made into cabinets for a winery-themed entertaining space. It is these original, customized built-ins that make a house a home.

Participating in the annual HomeAid Atlanta Project Playhouse 2006 allowed the firm to give back to the community. The Kritkos designed a small-scale replica of the oldest courthouse in Atlanta, originally built in 1825. Sharing this piece of history with the youth of today, Country Classic Builders donated its time, talent and materials in the construction of its contribution, which raised funds benefiting HomeAid Atlanta. The "playhouse" received five distinguished awards from the Greater Atlanta Home Builders Association, acknowledging the duo who joyfully share their gift of custom homebuilding every day.

COUNTRY CLASSIC BUILDERS, INC.

George Kritko

Vicki Kritko

PO Box 475

Tyrone, GA 30290

404.871.1957

f: 770.631.4757

www.countryclassicbuilders.com

ABOVE LEFT:
Arched Palladian windows shed light on an elegant foyer showcasing a graceful, curved and flaired stairway. White oak with inlaid walnut floors, wainscoting, mouldings and columns add classical European details. Interior design by Vicki Kritko.
Photograph by John Umberger

ABOVE RIGHT:
The gourmet kitchen overlooks a lakeside golf course reflecting its natural colors; the green antique-glazed cabinetry and center island are crafted from poplar and are complemented by honed granite counters and a deep farm-style sink. Interior design by Lynn Mock of Monet Gardens.
Photograph by John Umberger

FACING PAGE:
A European-style kitchen functions beautifully with burgundy-glazed island, custom desk space and cabinetry with pull-outs and polished granite countertops. The flowing floor plan features a breakfast/beverage bar that is perfect for family parties. Interior design by Vicki Kritko.
Photograph by John Umberger

ROB MARETT
Rob Marett Custom Homes

Bob Marett Sr. put his heart and soul into building homes in Georgia. Bob was always Rob Marett's professional mentor and as a young boy Rob started in the business helping his dad around various building sites and working each summer throughout high school. Rob soon became enthused about the building business, just like his father, and decided to follow in his footsteps, continuing his legacy. Bob is now retired and three generations of the Marett family live on the Atlantic coast's renowned St. Simons Island, which boasts the top five-star resort in America, The Lodge at Sea Island Golf Club.

After graduating from the University of Georgia having majored in American history, Rob returned to his hometown of Atlanta and rejoined his father in the family business. They started working together in 1991 and had been building homes for 10 years when Rob decided to embark on a new adventure, opening the doors of Rob Marett Custom Homes in 2001. Exclusively building custom and speculative residences, his team of project supervisors, carpenters and tradesmen has constructed luxurious private homes throughout neighborhoods in Atlanta, Reynolds

Plantation and Sea Island. When partnered with his father, they also built many distinguished traditional residences in Buckhead, Sandy Springs and Dunwoody.

Rob is now dedicating his firm to building single-family primary residences and second-home cottages on the waterfront, marshlands and inland areas throughout beautiful St. Simons Island and Sea Island. Rob is currently building in Sea Island's exclusive 3,000-acre Frederica development featuring lakeside and marsh properties, on Sea Island and in Old Seaside at The Lodge. These most impressive homes have dramatic floor plans and elevations designed by renowned local Sea Island and Atlanta architects. Some of Rob's custom-built homes have been featured in national publications including *House Beautiful*, *Southern Living* and *Golf Digest* magazines.

Most recently recognized as the ultimate golf residence, Rob is building the *Golf Digest* 2007 showcase home in prestigious Reynolds Plantation on Lake Oconee. The lower level of this sprawling 9,800-square-foot residence has its own interactive golf simulator, golf fitness area designed for the avid golfer, an indoor and outdoor putting green, outdoor swimming pool with adjoining spa, media room and a state-of-the-art wine cellar and humidor.

LEFT:
This custom residence on picturesque Strom Thurmond Lake offers relaxed living with a hand-crafted natural stone fireplace and impressive floor-to-ceiling window views. Architecture by William T. Baker & Associates.
Photograph by Tria Giovann

FACING PAGE:
This private residence integrated into the wooded landscape in Reynolds Plantation features natural stone patio and terrace for elegant outdoor entertaining, especially poolside at dusk. Architecture by TS Adams Studio, Inc.
Photograph by Gil Stose

One of the most unusual and challenging construction projects that Rob has been involved with was an estate home that incorporated a unique radius glass tower framed in steel with bronze cladding with a radius glass clerestory on top. The tower also featured a free-standing natural limestone staircase and amenities including a sophisticated wine cellar below and a planted palm tree as the centerpiece.

Specializing in strictly new custom home construction, Rob appreciates the intrinsic beauty of the land and seaside property available on St. Simons Island and Sea Island as it presents a perfect backdrop for his one-of-a-kind residences. Living and working on St. Simons Island is a wonderful experience and his wife, Braden, and their three children love the coastal lifestyle. As a builder of integrity in the area and being a full-time resident he stays close to the needs of his clients with a full understanding of their desires, always maintaining the highest standards for the communities he serves.

TOP LEFT:
This welcoming private residence in Dunwoody exudes a European feel and is a well-crafted home of brick and stone with weathered copper details and complex roofline. Architecture by Harrison Design Associates.
Photograph courtesy of Rob Marett Custom Homes

BOTTOM LEFT:
Country cottage influence is evident in this charming Strom Thurmond Lake custom residence. Architecture by William T. Baker & Associates.
Photograph courtesy of Rob Marett Custom Homes

FACING PAGE:
This custom country home with a large second-story porch combines a cedar shingle and natural stone exterior reflecting the quiet serenity of the neighborhood, located in Madison, Georgia. Architecture by TS Adams Studio, Inc.
Photograph courtesy of Rob Marett Custom Homes

Rob enjoys his leisure time on the Island as an active sport fisherman, in both freshwater and saltwater lakes, as well as seasonal hunting. When he is not wearing fishing attire you may find him with his friends and clients playing a round of golf at one of the Sea Island golf courses. Enthusiastically reading architectural books, he is inspired today by the residential designs of Addison Mizner and Hays Town, studying stellar examples of their work as seen throughout Sea Island, Palm Beach and Louisiana. At the end of the day, Rob genuinely holds his father in the highest esteem, the one man who has been the most positive influence in his career.

ROB MARETT CUSTOM HOMES
Rob Marett
PO Box 21259
St. Simons Island, GA 31522
912.634.4588
f: 706.243.4817
www.robmarettcustomhomes.com

JUDY MOZEN

Handcrafted Homes, Inc.

The tale of two inner city school teachers turned custom homebuilders is a fascinating story. It all began with woman-power when Judy Mozen founded Handcrafted Homes, Inc. in 1976 after graduating from Agnes Scott College. With a political science, history and economics background and secondary education certificate, she decided to embark on an entrepreneurial venture into the male-dominated world of designing and building homes.

Several years later, Georgia native and University of Georgia graduate, Randy Urquhart, joined the one-woman shop, where he became lead superintendent. After working together for six years they found more in common than teaching and building. The couple married, blended families and has enjoyed more than 20 years as dynamic business partners.

This wife-husband team advantage helps them relate well to prospective custom home buyers because they have a better understanding of the needs of both buyers. One surprising role reversal is that Judy is often on the job site

in her blue jeans, while Randy is in the office handling financial aspects of each design-build project. Projects flow smoothly thanks to Judy's creative design vision, listening skills and primary focus on job-site details combined with Randy's patience and client-builder rapport. Making clients happy and having a "proud to serve" enthusiasm is the motivating force for Judy, Randy and the entire team at Handcrafted Homes, Inc. This work ethic exemplified in every home has earned the firm designation as a Certified Professional Home Builder from the Greater Atlanta Home Builders Association. Judy is also a Certified Remodeler, a notable distinction, from the National Association of the Remodeling Industry.

They design and build in metro Atlanta and the North Georgia Mountains in a variety of styles from Southwestern to ultra traditional, Victorian to ultra modern, Craftsman, as well as Asian and European influences. Whether receiving plans from an architect or drawing them on her own, Judy finds it thrilling to watch a home design become a reality. The firm's original, award-winning work is a labor of love ranging from million-dollar custom homes to smaller renovation projects. Much of the company's work is repeat business with lifelong clients who want new homes as their lives evolve from young families into their retirement years.

FACING PAGE LEFT:
This stunning front entry, surrounded by curved soffits and high glass windows, introduces one to the contemporary architecture that flows throughout the home.
Photograph by John Umberger

FACING PAGE RIGHT:
A mosaic stone inlay surrounded by four built-in corner perfumeries creates a circular focal point leading to the different functional areas of this master bath.
Photograph by John Umberger

RIGHT:
Mahogany cabinets and cherry flooring create warmth in this traditional kitchen, which features a mahogany arched alcove passageway, thus allowing for a continuous flow of cabinetry.
Photograph by John Umberger

For Judy and Randy, success is first a commitment to each individual client but also to the community as a whole. They regularly devote time to non-profit groups in urban Atlanta as a way to give back. Judy's philanthropic contributions have included fundraising for Habitat for Humanity and Atlanta Technical College, and she is an active member of Leadership Atlanta working on the city's key issues.

To recharge their creative minds year-round, they escape to their solar-powered, rustic mountain cabin amidst nature minus most creature comforts. It is this balanced lifestyle that keeps them grounded and in touch with their diverse Atlanta clientele, providing gold-star guidance to each and every one with positive professionalism and a belief that "attitude is everything."

TOP RIGHT:
The playful architecture and its bold colors create a relaxing yet stimulating experience in this media room.
Photograph by Warren Bond Sr.

BOTTOM RIGHT:
Curved architecture, accented by dramatic indirect lighting and 30-foot-high grand arches, creates the exciting ambience of this contemporary home.
Photograph by Warren Bond Sr.

FACING PAGE:
Floors of ebonized walnut inlaid with travertine, paired with dramatic mouldings and arches, make one's journey through this home gallery a visual feast.
Photograph by Erica George Dines

HANDCRAFTED HOMES, INC.
Judy Mozen
Randy Urquhart
505 Boulder Way
Roswell, GA 30075
770.642.1010
f: 770.642.4110
www.handcraftedhomes-inc.com

CHIP MURRAH
Chip Murrah Architect

Classical architecture is never boring when Chip Murrah is involved. His designs take on a fresh, traditional flavor, as he transforms ideas into floor plans filled with open spaces and a multitude of windows for maximum light, higher ceilings for spaciousness and natural materials for an open and bright feeling. Creating traditional residential architecture, combined with the conveniences of a modern lifestyle, is Chip's forte.

Atlanta-born, Chip interned with one of the foremost classical architects in Atlanta while earning his architectural degree from Georgia Tech. Inspired by all that he was taught and exposed to, Chip continued on to receive his Master of Architecture degree, establishing his own studio in 1990. His list of credentials and achievements are many, some of which include being a registered architect licensed in Georgia and a member of NCARB. His residential designs have been featured in national and local publications such as *Atlanta Custom Homes*, *Atlanta Homes & Lifestyles* and *Better Homes and Gardens* magazines.

Chip's homes reflect a Southern style. He gives his imprint to each design by incorporating grand porches and majestic columns, which evoke a quality that will still look current 20 years from now. These timeless designs are elements rooted in Classicism and are perfect for historical urban neighborhoods including famed Buckhead, Brookhaven and the elegant Sandy Springs communities.

He also has expertise designing historically accurate renovations and additions for Atlanta's turn-of-the-century neighborhoods. Building upon what is already there, improving the exterior, expanding an interior, updating and reworking are challenges that he welcomes. He thrives on taking a well-built home, re-engineering it and designing additions to accommodate the changing needs of the homeowners.

TOP LEFT:
A beautifully designed Charleston-style home in Kennesaw, Georgia, offers Southern charm and easy living.
Photograph by Jodi Dybowski, Fly Design Inc.

BOTTOM LEFT:
The early 20th-century-style custom library showcases classic mahogany paneling and built-in bookcases, wood-grid coffered ceiling, detailed custom fireplace mantel with green marble surround and exquisite hardwood flooring.
Photograph by Woody Williams

FACING PAGE:
This custom-designed, traditional-style home with Mission influences in Kennesaw, Georgia, features inviting wraparound porches characteristic of Southern architecture.
Photograph by Jodi Dybowski, Fly Design Inc.

Ideas begin on paper and are then developed into renderings for presentation. His clients are of various ages and backgrounds, most with a good understanding of their needs. Chip's clients are savvy. He remarks, "It's almost too easy." Families come to his firm with an appreciation for traditional architecture and know most of what they want. Atlanta has a long history of beautiful homes rich with design that inspire people to build new, second homes as their lives evolve.

With a passion for international travel, Chip brings a wealth of ideas to the table and this knowledge influences his designs. He incorporates elements such as creating an outdoor courtyard space with European flair, an intimate fireplace based on a centuries-old villa and exquisite Old World details—all of which are integrated into the classical style of architecture and unique to his work.

TOP LEFT:
This custom French-country private residence was designed for a respected local builder and interior designer.
Photograph by Jodi Dybowski, Fly Design Inc.

BOTTOM LEFT:
This custom, Southern-traditional home in Kennesaw, Georgia, features a gracious entrance with stately columns and brick with natural stone exterior.
Photograph by Jodi Dybowski, Fly Design Inc.

FACING PAGE:
A custom gambrel-style home in Newnan, Georgia is an inviting place with Southern charm.
Photograph by Neil Dent Studios

There are many impressive home designs, including one on an estate in Newnan complete with a stretch of forest and a lake. He designed an impressive gambrel-style home with several outbuildings to take advantage of this countryside landscape. The homeowner couple was a rare interior designer and craftsman team—the Arts-and-Crafts interior was a showcase for his handcrafted woodwork as well as her finishing touches with the end result remarkable both inside and out.

Chip Murrah designs up to 50 new custom residences and renovations per year, which keeps him active, but his family life is where his heart is. He treasures his free time simply unwinding with his family and trusty golden retriever Pal, but, most of all, he enjoys horseback riding with his wife, Jodi, and young equestrian daughter, Virginia, on beautiful Georgia trails.

CHIP MURRAH ARCHITECT
Chip Murrah
1915 Airport Road, Suite 2J
Atlanta, GA 30341
404.848.0013
f: 404.848.0013

YONG PAK
CHARLES HEYDT

Pak Heydt & Associates, LLC

Specializing in traditional and classical architecture with a modern sensibility, Pak Heydt & Associates is one of Atlanta's most distinguished architectural firms. The firm designs custom residences for discerning patrons who desire exquisite craftsmanship, the highest quality of materials and a distinct home of enduring legacy.

An expansion of the architectural firm Yong Pak founded in 1997, Pak Heydt & Associates was formed when Charles Heydt became a partner in 2003. Prior to establishing their firm, both partners cultivated their in-depth knowledge and understanding of classical architecture through prestigious academic programs, individual travels to Europe, England and the Middle East and practical work experience in an established Atlanta architectural firm.

Recognized for providing exceptional personalized attention, the team works closely with clients to determine the architectural style best suited to their desires and lifestyle while integrating modern comforts for luxurious living. The

firm creates an original home within an authentic architectural language reflective of its client's desires, at times drawing inspiration from the client's furniture and collections.

Pak Heydt believes in architectural authenticity and the importance of absorbing historical precedence. The firm's mastery of American, English and European vernacular and classical styles is evident in the breadth of its work. Projects range from Colonial, Grecian and Shingle to Georgian, Tudor and Elizabethan, as well as the distinctive European regional styles of Normandy, Provence and Tuscany. They are dedicated to creatively accomplishing the client's program while adhering to the distinguishing characteristics and nuances of the desired vernacular.

Regardless of stylistic differences, Pak Heydt designs each home to integrate with its particular site, taking advantage of natural features or harmonizing with the scale of the neighboring homes. Additionally, the firm strives to create unique spaces. Interior room layouts are planned with care to provide plenty of natural light and a strong connection to the outdoors, while courtyards and loggias are created to provide comfortable, private exterior rooms.

RIGHT:
A Tudor-inspired limestone portal creates an entrance to this English-style house.
Photograph by Brie Williams

FACING PAGE LEFT:
The antique French oak doors and wrought-iron balcony rail are incorporated in a new cast stone overdoor of French Classicism.
Photograph by Erica George Dines

FACING PAGE RIGHT:
Scamozzi pilasters and a broken pediment are carved in limestone for an early Georgian entrance.
Photograph by Jeff Herr

Pak Heydt residences are renowned for their craftsmanship and refined elements. Impeccable attention to detail is revealed in the seamless integration of antiques, mantels, doors, ironwork, flooring and other architectural artifacts. Drawing on its experience, education and travels, the accomplished team fastidiously delineates all architectural aspects of a home, including: exterior walls, porticos, bays, balustrades, interior millwork, cabinetry, paneling, ceilings, mantels, stair halls and custom furniture.

TOP:
A charming living porch conceals a garage opposite a courtyard garden from the main house.
Landscape architecture by John Howard.
Photograph by Erica George Dines

BOTTOM LEFT:
Living room and library have been combined to create this dramatic yet comfortable two-story room paneled in brown oak. Interior design by Susan Lapelle.
Photograph by Jeff Herr

BOTTOM RIGHT:
A breakfast room is created with the feel of a garden pavilion.
Photograph by Erica George Dines

FACING PAGE:
A family home in the tradition of Tidewater, Virginia, is carefully crafted of handmade brick and custom millwork.
Photograph by Jeff Herr

The exquisite craftsmanship of each home's construction is a signature of Pak Heydt. Each component is individually designed to contribute to a harmonious whole. A feeling of timelessness is conveyed with materials of uncompromising quality and durability, many of which are antique or reclaimed. Stone and brick are detailed to emphasize their richness and permanence, interior mouldings are custom milled, staircases are graced with handcrafted balustrades and iron railings are hand-wrought.

TOP:
This charming and inviting entrance hall welcomes guests to this residence with a fireplace opposite the front door, a warm textured stone floor and French doors to the terrace. Interior design by Jacquelynne P. Lanham.
Photograph by Erica George Dines

BOTTOM:
This family room and kitchen addition combines traditional elements with rustic materials for a casual family environment.
Photograph by Jeff Herr

FACING PAGE:
The rear of this house is a picturesque composition of gabled and hipped roofs, stone and brick, windows and loggia. Garden design by Brooks Garcia.
Photograph by Jeff Herr

Encouraging its clients to invest in longevity, materials of the highest quality, superior construction and the integration of energy-conscious technology provide the foundation upon which Pak Heydt builds a legacy for the next generation.

With its residential designs and renovations featured in national and regional magazines including *Veranda*, *Southern Accents* and *Atlanta Homes & Lifestyles*, Pak Heydt is committed to designing unique traditional and classical residences of exceptional quality and distinction.

RIGHT:
Eighteenth-century paneling and a marble mantel were imported from France to create this dining room. The oak parquet de Versailles was created on site. Interior design by Ginny Magher.
Photograph by Erica George Dines

FACING PAGE:
The grand scale and symmetry of this façade are relieved by forward protecting wings, mullioned windows and the texture of painted brick. Landscape architecture by John Howard.
Photograph by Erica George Dines

PAK HEYDT & ASSOCIATES, LLC
Yong Pak
Charles Heydt
345 Peachtree Hills Avenue, Suite 500
Atlanta, GA 30305
404.231.3195
f: 404.231.3193
www.pakheydt.com

ZORAN PERICIC

Zoran Design Associates

A true artist, philosopher, architect and master draftsman, Zoran Pericic arrived from his home country of Croatia in 1989 with the dream of living and working in America. He graduated from the University of Architecture in Zagreb and practiced commercial and residential architectural design for nine years in Europe. His sincere desire for a new experience and opportunity in the United States became a reality; he moved to Atlanta and began working for firms in both commercial and residential design, learning the market and making new friends.

Inspired by the beautiful, classical architecture of historic Atlanta, Zoran soon realized he wanted to specialize in custom residential design as it was closer to his abilities and interests. He had the privilege of working for some of the most respected architectural firms in the city and gleaned professional knowledge and experience on American soil. He officially established Zoran Design Associates architectural studio in 2001 and has been designing high-end residences for his discerning clientele ever since.

During his childhood, Zoran was an observer of the beauty in nature with an innate artistic ability who loved drawing, sketching and building classical scale-model ships. His passion for working with his hands, building intricate models, extreme patience and eye for detail was destined to be meaningful in whatever profession he decided upon.

As a registered architect in Europe practicing in Atlanta, he brings his highly original approach of hand-drafted designs, freehand schematic sketches and marker renderings to each and every architectural project. He is a true artist who takes thoughts and images, translating the feeling through his favorite blue pencil or extra-fine ink pen—convinced it makes all of the difference in his designs. Designing with "soul" and tracking ideas on paper, taking drawings into three-dimensional live studies is characteristic of Zoran's unique mindset. He is a thinker and has been most influenced by revered Renaissance artists Michelangelo Buonarotti and Leonardo da Vinci. Studying great masters who had discipline and worked tirelessly, loving and nurturing their creations, is Zoran's own philosophy. It is his firm's mission statement that fuels his work with four elements to the creative process: admiration, desire, curiosity and courage. Having courage to make something new or different is what stimulates his creative expression, and it shows in his remarkable interior plans and exterior designs.

TOP LEFT:
A front façade perspective of this French Chateau country estate shows detailed wooden garage doors and artistic brick and stonework.
Photograph by John Umberger

BOTTOM LEFT:
This magnificent French-country villa in Alpharetta combines exterior materials including natural fieldstone, solid specialty brick, cedar shake shingles and standing seam copper roof.
Photograph by John Umberger

FACING PAGE:
The rear elevation of this French Chateau country estate integrates natural stone, a lagoon-style swimming pool, waterfall and jacuzzi spa.
Photograph by John Umberger

Good work is what genuinely matters, and Zoran values dedication over awards and accolades. He allows his work to speak for itself and his savvy clientele attest to the quality of his designs. Working as an architect rooted in classicism, he detests Kitsch. His home designs are like sculptures; a fresh new interpretation of classic form with a touch of drama and contrasts, avoiding overly repetitive elements or direct imitation of a given architectural style. His passion and energy are expressed throughout the design process and in the final construction of each residence. They are his masterpieces with a distinctive aesthetic quality, his signature. Just like a composer uses musical notes to write a symphonic arrangement, he takes architectural elements of style, rearranging them through the grammar of architecture in a new way to create a unique living experience.

Multifaceted, Zoran is an architect and talented artist who played piano as a child and is currently learning classical guitar, which has enlightened him to the true creative process. He applies these insights to every project. Modern, non-spiritual and empty architecture displease Zoran. He infuses each project with a feeling, challenging himself, seeking endless inspiration so the excitement is present at concept stage before any architectural plan can emerge.

TOP RIGHT:
The charming French-country villa in Alpharetta, Georgia, features a protected stone entrance, rustic window shutters and a cedar shake shingled roof to meld into the scenic, wooded site.
Photograph by John Umberger

BOTTOM RIGHT:
This Mediterranean renaissance villa in Alpharetta showcases hard European stucco, clay roof tiles and standing seam copper roof details to create a Tuscan influence.
Photograph by John Umberger

FACING PAGE:
This French country villa in Marietta, Georgia, boasts fieldstone and hard European stucco exterior facade, cast stone quoins, classical Tuscan columns and standing seam copper roof dormers.
Photograph by John Umberger

He cares for each client by seeking to understand their lifestyle and is sensitive to their needs, enabling them to discover their own "soul" through the process. He helps them articulate their own thoughts via his first schematic sketches, establishing communication early on. Many of his clients are young families and he works with developers and builders in the prestigious residential communities of Tiller Walk, River's Call, Citadella and Ellard. Designing several new residences per year, his multimillion-dollar homes reflect his European heritage. He designs homes reminiscent of charming Tuscan villas, elegant country French-chateaus, English Manor homes and a variety of classical styles. Using fieldstone, Old World beam work and elements of impact, his homes stimulate the senses. His European influence is evident in every home, and he achieves a timeless look and feel by his thorough understanding of materials versus style, versus detail. Adeptly integrating his designs into the context of an environment, he sets the tone with high-end elegance yet his constructions dramatically stand out amidst their settings. He designs a home with relevance to the play of light over the structure, what direction the home is facing and with regard to interesting outdoor topography like creeks and woodlands.

TOP LEFT:
This Italian renaissance villa in Atlanta has an exterior façade that combines brick, cast stone quoins and cast stone Tuscan pilasters for a dramatic, stately effect.
Photograph by John Umberger

BOTTOM LEFT:
This authentic English countryside residence in Marietta, Georgia, showcases natural field stone, brick work and standing seam copper roof details.
Photograph by John Umberger

FACING PAGE:
A charming Swiss country villa in Marietta, Georgia, this home displays a creative use of natural fieldstone, rustic earth-toned brick, cedar beams and standing seam copper swoop roof details.
Photograph by John Umberger

Zoran returns to his native country on the breathtaking blue Adriatic each year for active seaside relaxation to revitalize his work. He is also an experienced alpine skier who travels to the European slopes each winter. His lively sense of humor and playful nature are key to his creative work, as his intuitive designs evolve from a spontaneous and imaginative mind. At the end of the day, this Renaissance man quietly peruses his beloved books on the life and works of two colossal geniuses, Michelangelo and Leonardo, for pure classical inspiration and energy. He lives by the great master's words, which are printed on his business card: "Where the spirit doesn't work with a hand, there is no art." —Leonardo da Vinci

ZORAN DESIGN ASSOCIATES
Zoran Pericic
Atlanta, GA
770.319.9805

JOHN R. RENTZ
John R. Rentz Architect

On St. Simons Island just off of Georgia's Atlantic coast lives one of the area's foremost residential architects. John R. Rentz, AIA, founded his practice in 1981 after training and graduating from Auburn University School of Architecture in 1977, where he earned his bachelor's degree in environmental science and an advanced degree in architecture.

A small-town boy, growing up in Colquitt, Georgia, he was drawn to the ocean and after college relocated to live on the Georgia coast. With seaside, marshland and inland properties perfect for his residential designs, St. Simons Island offers John many wonderful opportunities to do his best work designing multimillion-dollar custom residences and renovating the many historical cottages along the seaboard.

LEFT:
Interiors meld to the numerous outdoor spaces—the pool, spa, terrace, veranda and balconies—all of which reflect the importance of the relationship between interior and exterior.
Photograph by Attic Fire Architecture

The area continues to evolve with a strong contingent dedicated to protecting trees, the environment and sense of village established in St. Simons Island. More than being an architect, John has made a commitment to civic involvement, designing homes to integrate into the natural beauty of the island. To John, the field of architecture is a special profession where one has great influence and responsibility, setting standards of design quality with attention to the environment.

John is on the Advisory Board to the Village Master Plan and the St. Simons Island Land Trust where he is very involved in the organization's preservation efforts. He is also a member of the Coastal Georgia Historical Society, Georgia Historical Society and Georgia Trust for Historic Preservation, and has received two state awards for renovations of historic commercial buildings. John R. Rentz custom-designed residences have been featured in *Luxury Homes* and *Veranda* magazines.

John responds to clients' needs and allows the designs to reflect their desires in a tailored and polished manner. He has always been faithful to "realize his client's wishes, not his own," and this is his core philosophy. His loyal clients find the team experience of working with John to be a pleasurable and virtually effortless process.

TOP LEFT:
The marsh, river and sky define this interior space.
Photograph by Attic Fire Architecture

BOTTOM LEFT:
Design diversity is the trademark of the firm, exemplified by the more casual, nature-inspired "au natural" warmth found in this kitchen design, developed for a client with totally different needs and tastes.
Photograph by Attic Fire Architecture

FACING PAGE:
Successful architectural design is achieved when all elements, large or small, are experienced in a home—reflected in this ironwork gate as one departs or enters.
Photograph by Attic Fire Architecture

Designing in a variety of architectural expressions, an important common thread is John's emphasis on the indoor-outdoor relationship in a residential design. He incorporates vistas as well as personal courtyard views and places to rest such as verandas, loggias and porches. One feature of his designs is joining public space to private space, creating a "transition" space as he calls it. He designs passages and vestibules, interfaces and interesting places to display great art or an heirloom chest, making the home feel more logical, yet flowing. Designs reveal open floor plans with colonnades and arches to separate living spaces and rooms— fluid plans with true classical elements. John considers himself a classicist and is sensitive to traditional design elements. His designs incorporate true classical motifs from the fireplace mantel to mouldings, over-the-door treatments and use of materials. His designs range from elegant, understated Georgians to inviting lodge-like homes and Italian-inspired villas.

John is passionate about being an architect for the sheer joy of artistic expression and shares this same passion when creating his original oil paintings. Above all, he feels blessed by the sincere client friendships he forms and his fulfilling family life.

JOHN R. RENTZ ARCHITECT
John R. Rentz, AIA
Plantation House
300 Main Street, Suite 202
St. Simons Island, GA 31522
912.638.4952
f: 912.638.9696

MICHAEL ROBINSON

Michael Robinson Homes, Inc.

Born and raised in the granite-rich historic city of Stone Mountain, Michael Robinson is a lifelong native of Georgia and an established custom home builder who loves doing what he does best in the Atlanta locale and throughout the state he calls home. An ambitious teenager, Michael began working each summer during high school for a relative in the construction business where he caught the homebuilding fever.

Majoring in finance with a minor in real estate from Georgia State University, Michael took his first job building starter homes for a local company. It was here that he learned the basic business of construction within the Atlanta housing market for several years before founding his entrepreneurial custom home building firm in 1996.

Now with 17 years of solid experience he has become one of the Atlanta area's outstanding, award-winning custom home builders. He loves the brisk pace of building and completing up to 20 homes per year because he is able to see tangible results from his work, which keeps him growing professionally. Finishing a home to deliver a client's dream,

learning something new from each building experience and improving upon the next project are his driving motivations.

Most of all, Michael and his seasoned site superintendents work to create a truly custom home for each client that is both beautiful and livable, inside and out. He creates exteriors using unique combinations of natural stone, brick and cedar and believes it is the deliberate mix of materials which makes a home "uniquely yours," as their motto goes. His custom homes have an English Tudor and Craftsman-style design influence with a keen eye towards integrating modern trends such as exterior trim color and detail work.

Michael Robinson is an entrepreneurial custom home builder and takes professional pride in each and every home he creates. In fact, he builds each home as though he were building it for his very own family, in terms of overall quality and craftsmanship, with interior floor plans ahead of the curve to fit busy suburban lifestyles. Kitchens are king with separate keeping rooms finished with rough-sawn cedar beams to reflect the same feel of an exterior, and master bedrooms become personal retreats with wood-burning fireplaces and stack stone features to create warmth in a space.

TOP LEFT:
Well-crafted millwork and refined hardwood cabinetry are central to this rich gourmet kitchen accented with polished granite countertops and coordinating ceramic tile backsplash.
Photograph courtesy of Michael Robinson Homes, Inc.

BOTTOM LEFT:
Natural stone, multi-toned bricks, charming shutters and an arched double-door entry create a country cottage feeling perfectly suited to the wooded site in this custom home community.
Photograph courtesy of Michael Robinson Homes, Inc.

FACING PAGE:
This classic and elegant living room features built-in cabinetry, floor-to-ceiling windows, natural hardwood floors and an exquisite fireplace with marble hearth and surround.
Photograph courtesy of Michael Robinson Homes, Inc.

Michael beams with honor to have received prestigious Gold professionalism awards from the Greater Atlanta Home Builders Association. His work has been showcased in professional trade journals including *Today's Custom Homes*. Beyond professional recognition it is the company's mission to fulfill each homebuyer's vision with the ultimate goal in mind to deliver a one-of-a-kind, customized home that will truly enhance each special family's lifestyle.

MICHAEL ROBINSON HOMES, INC.
Michael Robinson
9015 Coventry Pointe
Suwanee, GA 30024
770.205.1536
f: 770.205.2394
www.michaelrobinsonhomesinc.com

DUANE STONE
Duane Stone & Associates, Inc.

"We take extreme delight in the details," says an inspired Duane Stone. With more than 25 years of practice, Duane is a respected designer specializing in custom homes, one-of-a-kind speculative houses and small-scale commercial projects. His business partner, Richard Hall, is a respected registered architect whose background further enhances the firm. Duane attended The College of Architecture at Georgia Institute of Technology for undergraduate and post-graduate work. He worked for larger commercial firms in Atlanta for three years in between his undergraduate and post-graduate studies, but his passion has always been designing homes. What began as freelance work became the current creative studio of Duane Stone & Associates, Inc., which he founded in 1989 and incorporated in 1993.

A classicist, Duane's greatest influences include renowned local architects Neil Reed and Philip Shutze, as well as English architects Sir Edwin Lutyens and Sir John Soane. London is his favorite city due to its energy, great architectural history

LEFT:
The beautiful stone terrace and classically inspired pool and spa are the highlight of the many outdoor rooms in the elegant, yet casual home.
Photograph by James Klotz

and exciting culture. His interests are not limited to English architecture, however, and he has experienced great professional pleasure in designing French, Italian, American classical and modern architecture.

Duane, an Atlanta native, appreciates his city as a fast-growing and exciting place where people are open to new ideas and design possibilities. At the same time, Atlanta is also a city that is residentially grounded in tradition. Duane's projects are often for infill situations in existing, stately Atlanta neighborhoods such as Buckhead, where traditional architecture is the norm. Duane believes that it is paramount to respect the existing character of an established area. Residences must be of appropriate scale and proportion, not only in relation to their specific style, but also in relation to the community as a whole. The firm's traditional work is far from tedious or unimaginative, understanding that his clients prefer not to live in "museums."

Designing 15 to 20 projects a year, Duane's hand touches each project. This ensures that nothing is ever lost in translation and each project goes out the door with the initial concept intact and the appropriate details realized. The firm's design work includes 75 percent new construction, 20 percent renovation and five percent commercial projects. Although many of the firm's projects are large, single-family homes in classic Atlanta neighborhoods, the firm's work is not limited to urban areas and Duane's design opportunities are quite involved and varied.

LEFT:
This beautiful floating Louis XIV-style staircase is highlighted by ironwork designed by Duane and forged by a European craftsman.
Photograph by James Klotz

FACING PAGE:
The grand living room is 22 feet by 40 feet, yet very intimate, and is accented by hand-hewn beams and a massive 16th-century limestone fireplace.
Photograph by James Klotz

Several recent projects are clear examples of the scope of firm. The first of these recent projects is the design of two H. Stockton men's apparel stores. One of these retail spaces features a very modern and exciting interior to entice a younger and more hip customer while not alienating the store's existing traditional clientele. Another unique design project is a series of single-family resort homes located within a master-planned community in National Village at Grand National in Opelika, Alabama, near Auburn University. These Craftsman cottage-style homes range in size from 1,800 to 3,500 square feet. They are much more casual and open than a traditionally large home to complement the relaxed resort lifestyle of this community.

Duane's adopted design philosophy is that "God is in the details." He firmly believes that if the design concept is good but the details are not executed properly, a project will not fulfill its potential. It will fall short of its possibilities.

TOP RIGHT:
This French Normandy-style home showcases many beautiful materials such as antique heart-pine doors, antique ironwork, a stately limestone door surround and steeply pitched slate roof.
Photograph by James Klotz

BOTTOM RIGHT:
Charming, hand-finished cabinetry, an oak island, marble and soapstone countertops and a marble mosaic backsplash with an inset of antique Delft tiles are all part of a successful Country French kitchen. Interior design by Duane Stone.
Photograph by James Klotz

FACING PAGE:
This majestic English manor home is situated on four beautifully terraced, park-like acres.
Photograph by James Klotz

The firm's forte includes the use of architectural antiques and bits of found history in its projects. These uncommon architectural details appear throughout its designs because of Duane's artful eye and treasure-hunting expertise. In his travels throughout the United States and Europe, he collects potential pieces that will find a home in one of his future designs. Whether it is the perfect antique chandelier, an unusual piece of carved wood, antique tiles or a period French mantelpiece, he will discover the architectural details and bring them home to be incorporated into his residential designs.

One of the most intimate projects that this firm has chosen to embrace is the personal residence of Duane's parents. This new home fulfills his mother's lifelong dream of living in a Country French home in beautiful Buckhead. Years were spent designing and collecting architectural antiques; two pairs of antique French doors and three antique French mantels. Expertly crafted in the French Normandy style, many patrons on a recent tour of homes were surprised to learn that the home was entirely new construction and not a renovation of an older historic home.

However, his treasures are not limited to antiquities. French-inspired hardware was selected as the finishing touch on the doors, windows and cabinetry throughout one client's home. Duane introduced

the clients to one of the world's premier restoration hardware manufacturers located in New York City. He personally commissioned hand-cast, hand-chaste and antique-finished 24-carat gold-plated hardware to create a historically authentic look. This same project also included a special Louis XIV finial and 60 medallions to grace its elegant stairway.

In addition to architecture, Duane's leisure interests include collecting or creating art, antiquing and gardening. These interests are all a reflection of a deep passion for design. "Design influences everything I do," says Duane.

TOP RIGHT:
A luxurious sweeping front lawn and expansive circular driveway complement this imposing, brick and stone English Manor estate home.
Photograph by James Klotz

BOTTOM RIGHT:
The courtyard entrance of this stately European Manor home incorporates a splendid mix of stone, old brick and limestone.
Photograph by James Klotz

FACING PAGE:
Antique mirrored French doors were the found object that inspired the detail in this Country French library, which leads to a comfortable living room.
Photograph by James Klotz

DUANE STONE & ASSOCIATES, INC.
Duane Stone
2200 Century Parkway, Suite 990
Atlanta, GA 30345
404.325.4907
f: 404.248.0966
www.duanestone.com

D. CLAY ULMER
H. ANNE BLAKELY SCIARRONE
JAMES E. CARSON JR.
ALLISON H. SUAZO

NCG Architects, Inc.

ABOVE:
With its reclaimed chestnut flooring, hand-hewn antique beams and warm plaster finishes, the living area of this residence exudes the irresistible charm and comfort of Tuscany. The owner's collection of Italian antiques and decorative items complements the authentically crafted interior.
Photograph by Rion Rizzo, Creative Sources Photography

FACING PAGE:
Reflecting its owner's Italian heritage, "Villa Sopravalle," is an Atlanta residence that draws heavily on Tuscan architectural influences.
Photograph by Rion Rizzo, Creative Sources Photography

Known for its resort and residential work for over 35 years, Atlanta-based NCG Architects, Inc. is a vital, second-generation firm continuing the legacy of its founders. This dynamic firm is led by six principals having the collective experience and professional credentials to continue the stellar work of the originally established team. By consistently providing high-end architectural designs, NCG Architects has paved its way into producing prestigious clubhouses, luxury condominium addresses and grand private residences throughout the Southeast as well as developments in Ireland, Spain, Bermuda and Italy.

From stately beach cottages on Sea Island and Tuscan-inspired villas to condominiums that reflect European manor homes, the team is well-versed designing in the classical style for clients who are drawn to and have a preference for tradition. Their authentically detailed homes include Mid-Atlantic Colonial, Old English, Country French and Jeffersonian architectural styles, to name a few. Prior to each project, the team extensively researches the local

vernacular and visits the site, ensuring that the home is contextually appropriate within a region or historic neighborhood.

The firm has a rare depth of knowledge that stems from its members' vast experience in various design and construction techniques resulting from a wide array of project types. They transfer this mindset to each custom home design. Often interviewing builders for their clients, they frequently choose those that share their commercial experience because they understand what it takes to produce enduring structures. The architectural team draws on ideas from history, reinterpreting elements to create new custom home designs unique to each client. They travel internationally, collecting reference materials and photographs to include in their ever-evolving library of historical architecture books. The firm is also keenly aware of the wealth of Atlanta architecture from the 1920s and 1930s and influenced by the work of Reid and Shutze, local notables of that era.

Members of the firm value the architect-client relationship and it is this joint "vision accomplished" attitude that moves them collaboratively through each project. Striving to create a home that is aesthetically pleasing, appropriate to its location and one that meets the client's needs is the ultimate goal of each design project. The firm has won

TOP LEFT:
The picturesque stucco and stone home is composed of strong interlocking volumes reminiscent of early 20th-century homes.
Photograph by Andrew Stivers, Bluetack Photography

BOTTOM LEFT:
The informal plan is carefully adapted to an eight-acre wooded site. This outdoor living room illustrates the home's strong relationship of interior and exterior spaces.
Photograph by Andrew Stivers, Bluetack Photography

FACING PAGE:
Taking advantage of its dramatic wooded hillside site, this private residence in Columbus recalls the grand axial schemes of classical European villas. The tile roof, stone colonnades, stone balustrades, marble floors, gardens, pools and fountains further enhance this traditional architectural statement of the Old World.
Photograph by Gabriel Benzur

numerous awards of distinction for architectural design including the *Southern Living* magazine's house of the year, American Resort Development Association recognition and a variety of awards for clubhouse design.

One 14,000-square-foot residence included a room designed to incorporate 100-year-old paneled walls from a foreign embassy that were disassembled, moved and reinstalled into the home. The team built an impressive room around this preserved piece of history to create a new space imbued with antiquity. Another owner requested that the house be modeled on authentic Tuscan villas. The resulting home led to what the partners consider to be their highest compliment, having an architect outside of the firm insist that the house must have been designed by an Italian architect.

The firm's architects have a shared affinity for refined classical design elements. Imagine a floating, cantilevered staircase, imported clay tiles wrapped around a conical tower or a sculpted family crest above a portico. These unique elements bespeak classic elegance and are representative of the uncommon details in a custom residence designed by this highly creative group of accomplished architects.

NCG ARCHITECTS, INC.
D. Clay Ulmer, AIA
H. Anne Blakely Sciarrone, AIA
James E. Carson Jr., AIA
James V. Hanna II, AIA
W. Philip Monk, AIA
Terry M. Tanner, AIA
Allison H. Suazo, AIA
730 Peachtree Street, Suite 800
Atlanta, GA 30308
404.892.4510
f: 404.892.6424
www.ncgarch.com

CLARENCE VINSON
GREGORY R. PORTMAN
BRETT SUNDERLAND
HAITHAM N. HADDAD

PFVS Architects, Inc.

As the director of design and a founding principal, Clarence Vinson, AIA, has masterminded the creative vision for one of Atlanta's preeminent architectural firms. PFVS Architects has flourished since its founding in 1987; many of Atlanta's corporate executives, sports celebrities, acclaimed athletes and high-profile entertainers have turned to this notable studio for excellence in creative residential design.

Visionary clients, talented staff and abundant resources make Atlanta an ideal home for the firm. Sensitive to the surroundings and site relationships unique to each project, this progressive team creates designs in diverse styles reflective of each client's personality. Setting egos aside, they listen intently to each client, learning about their preferences, lifestyle needs and desires. With a strong work ethic and shared values, PFVS truly cares about each individual client and endeavors to painstakingly implement their dreams during the fluid creative process from conceptual design to the last brush stroke of paint.

Raised in Macon, Georgia, Clarence graduated from the Georgia Institute of Technology in 1984, where he earned both his bachelor's degree and his Master of Architecture. During college Clarence immersed himself in the principles of classicism and learned to apply these time-proven principles with a modern influence. These developmental years also exposed him to environmentally sound ideas, including solar energy and the use of renewable resources, which are evident in his designs to this day. This solid formal education gave Clarence the classical architectural skills and technical expertise needed to excel, but it was not until shortly after college when his international trek through Germany, Switzerland, Italy and France enlightened him to the wondrous possibilities of his profession.

His innate love for drawing and demonstrated math aptitude during earlier school days coupled with his insatiable curiosity about buildings and construction led him to his life's work and passion. In high school he was certain about becoming an architect and obtained his first job with a local architect at age 17. Before college he studied Frank Lloyd Wright and became most inspired by his range of designs from residential to commercial architecture. Later, throughout his education, he grew to admire American contemporaries of commercial architecture including Argentine-born Cesar Pelli, Richard Alan Meier and the revered legend I.M. Pei, along with a

LEFT:
Cascading stairways lead from the upper lawn terrace to the pool area, with the master suite wing beyond.
Photograph by Thomas Watkins Photography

range of classical architects from the past. The firm's unique custom home designs exhibit a characteristic modern influence as well as what Clarence terms "eclectic traditional," a fresh interpretation of historical precedence, while interjecting the latest technologies, which is indicative of their varied range of styles. Clearly the firm is not defined by one architectural style.

Focused on new residential designs, Clarence has mastered the art of the quintessential "estate," designing custom homes in the countryside on larger properties, on the river with picturesque views and in the North Georgia Mountains with an occasional in-town project integrated within Atlanta's historic Buckhead community. Consistent client referrals are the norm and their residential projects include working exclusively on two or three projects during a year's time, as many of these residences are very customized and require intense commitments.

TOP RIGHT:
A view of the rear elevation is enjoyed across the expansive 300-foot-long pool.
Photograph by Thomas Watkins Photography

BOTTOM RIGHT:
The master bedroom looks out over pool and trellis/pavilion areas.
Photograph by Thomas Watkins Photography

One Italianate Neoclassical style multimillion-dollar home designed expressly for a sports celebrity is a spacious 55,000-square-foot estate. Upon entering this memorable home one encounters a formal dome-capped rotunda with clerestory windows flanked by a buttressed ceiling, a grand limestone and wrought-iron staircase in the center structure with two L-shaped wings forming the traditionally inspired compound. As with every project, the process begins with an initial look at the property with the client to examine the home's potential surroundings and its natural features. Sensitivity to the site's topography from river or lake, woods to hillside sets the ultimate design direction. They meet with the new homeowner, gathering not only programmatic needs of how they would like to use their new home, but also their favorite images of what appeals to them, gleaning a better understanding of the client's lifestyle, setting the stage for conceptual development. Creative hand-sketches are the first plans ever drawn, then on to marker image sketches, and finally photo-realistic renderings and computer-generated construction documents showing technical aspects and details needed for construction.

LEFT:
This grand hallway terminates at a trophy gallery replete with custom display cases.
Photograph by Thomas Watkins Photography

FACING PAGE LEFT:
Viewed from the open kitchen and overlooking the living area below is this delightfully contemporary dining area.
Photograph by Gary Knight & Associates

FACING PAGE RIGHT:
Clad in natural stone and lit by an exquisite chandelier, this gracious master bath suite is replete with much-enjoyed accoutrements.
Photograph by Gary Knight & Associates

From vibrant Atlanta to the waterfront on posh Palm Beach to Florida's Tampa Bay, the firm is renowned for working on both residential developments and commercial ventures. High-rise luxury condominiums and modern mixed-use buildings as well as multi-family complexes located in growing college towns show the design diversity of the firm. In addition to residential projects the award-winning firm is known for its large-scale hospitality/hotel and retail/office projects; this contributes directly to the success of its large-scale residential projects, as stronger and more durable materials are utilized.

Viewed by industry peers as a strong design studio—versus a production-oriented firm—its core design philosophy is based on the premise that "opposition" in architecture exists, and how one balances these elements defines art from mere buildings. Composing contrasting elements of light and dark, textures, form and space while being influenced by everything one sees, the firm designs an original interpretation of each unique situation. Assembling these diametrically opposed pieces, and creating a dynamic relationship between them, becomes an intangible aesthetic one can only experience.

PFVS ARCHITECTS, INC.

Clarence Vinson, AIA

Gregory R. Portman, AIA

Brett Sunderland, AIA

Haitham N. Haddad, AIA

5416 Glenridge Drive

Atlanta, GA 30342

404.503.5000

f: 404.503.5050

www.pfvs.com

ABOVE:
With forms and massing influenced by the English country estate classics, this lakeside home boasts garages and a private auto-court, which are hidden from view with the drive-under wing to the left.
Photograph by Gary Knight & Associates

FACING PAGE TOP:
Located above the main entry, the curvy balcony corridor has dual stairways that lead down to the living room.
Photograph by Gary Knight & Associates

FACING PAGE BOTTOM:
Views of this serene entry court are enjoyed from many of the interior spaces.
Photograph by Gary Knight & Associates

BOBBY WEBB SR.
JOSEPH BABB
BWC Properties LLC

This is a tale of a tennis pro and an airline captain turned professional homebuilders. After completing the ATP tennis tour and retiring from the airline profession these two long-time friends independently returned to their first passion of homebuilding and developing. Bobby Webb Sr. and Joseph Babb reunited while both building custom homes in Atlanta and were destined to become equal partners. In 2000 they joined their energies to form BWC Properties LLC. To add more muscle to the dynamic team, Bobby Webb Jr. has joined the firm as a certified residential construction superintendent from the National Association of Home Builders.

More than 30 years as Atlanta's premier homebuilders and developers, they have made a name for themselves in the upscale, historic Buckhead and prestigious Sandy Springs communities. Partnering together has been a fortuitous business journey but the key partnership is the one they hold with each client. It is their philosophy to be close business partners with each client in a true concerted effort to achieve exactly what they envision in their custom home, with the goal of exceeding expectations. Taking pride in its client's satisfaction is the firm's most important accolade.

The preeminent firm has also been professionally acknowledged in *The Atlanta Journal-Constitution* and *Atlanta Homes & Lifestyles* magazine. They are proud members of the National Association of Home Builders, the Georgia Association of Home Builders and the Greater Atlanta Home Builders Association.

The firm is known for building homes of European design with the flair and lifestyle indicative of the finest residences from France, Italy and England. Using authentic stonework and materials evoking this international style their work attracts clients from the diverse population in Atlanta. Building luxury homes in the multimillion-dollar bracket allows them to create residential structures featuring elements of style that are superior in workmanship and details. Cherry wood mouldings, rich paneling, custom hand rails with balusters and distinctive interior doors are all crafted on site using specialized equipment by one of their respected subcontractors.

At the early age of 12 Bobby drew the skyline of Atlanta and won the Atlanta Gaslight award for his renderings of the glittering city lights. This artistic expression signaled a brilliant future in business—today Bobby preserves the look and feel of Atlanta's famed historic neighborhoods and establishes new, traditional developments. It is Bobby's innate creativity complemented by Joseph's analytical mind and financial management experience that gives BWC the best of both worlds. Bobby's wife, Jennifer, a marketing and public relations

LEFT:
Overlooking the waterfall, water cascades into the spa and then into the pool surrounded by lush gardens.
Photograph by Robert Matta

FACING PAGE:
This signature kitchen has two islands, a custom-made stone cooking center with commercial equipment and a formal attached breakfast area.
Photograph by Robert Matta

professional, has been a source of inspiration and an enthusiastic supporter for their business. Joseph has a big-picture view as the pilot in the firm keeping an eye on the internal processes and each client's account. It is this core team and many loyal subcontractors that have made BWC Properties a powerhouse of talent.

Watching a home grow from concept through completion is pure excitement for the firm. The size of the custom homes they build presents unique challenges as most are over 12,000 square feet with complex, multilevel rooflines. Many are in-town homes and integrating them into the wooded landscape is something they have perfected. Beautiful Buckhead and Sandy Springs are known for their stately residences and BWC is known for building prime examples of classical, historically correct homes.

Expanding as developers, Joseph has brought the team to Colorado to build custom homes in Vail's ski country, creating majestic retreats for its clients. With steep mountain terrain and engineering

TOP LEFT:
This custom kitchen has two islands, a stone cooking center, convenient pot-filler and custom-milled heart pine flooring with planks varying up to 16 inches in width.
Photograph by Robert Matta

BOTTOM LEFT:
Cedar beams and Romanesque chandeliers accent this banquet-sized dining room warmed by a stone fireplace.
Photograph by Robert Matta

BOTTOM RIGHT:
A true French Country feeling is achieved with custom-made cedar shutters, decorative wrought-iron and gas lanterns.
Photograph by Robert Matta

FACING PAGE:
A grand circular staircase located inside the turret is accented with wrought-iron balusters and creates a stunning view inside and out.
Photograph by Robert Matta

obstacles they manage to build some of the most breathtaking vacation homes and primary residences. Whether building in Atlanta's Tiller Walk or Vail's Highland Meadows, they join with the most talented and respected architects in the field to create plans that are aesthetically outstanding and highly-detailed using quality construction techniques.

Achieving the "feeling" a client wants is first and foremost to BWC because it wants clients to be eager to come home each night. Characteristic of its homes are the signature interior woodwork and trim. They enjoy making dreams take shape for their clients and believe in the maxim that the "client is the boss." Their relationship with each homeowner is all about keeping them informed and providing personalized service. Listening to their clients, never sacrificing quality, meeting timelines and delivering on their promise is the success secret at BWC Properties.

BWC PROPERTIES LLC
Bobby Webb Sr.
Joseph Babb
206 Stewart Drive
Atlanta, GA 30342
404.273.7777
f: 404.851.9702
www.bwcproperties.com

JIM WILSON
Wilson & Dawson Architects

For more than 20 years, Jim Wilson, founder and principal of one of Atlanta's most-respected boutique studios, has practiced based on one philosophy: "Architecture is a process of translating thoughts into built form." His concept-driven and theoretical approach stems from formal architectural training at Tulane University and post-college architect experience in Boston and Manhattan. Jim worked with renowned American architect Peter Eisenman in New York City, where he was hugely influenced by the legend's theoretical methodology and contemporary thinking.

True to classical architecture and embracing these ideals, the firm designs residences based on classical principles in terms of scale and proportion, bringing an academic approach to what people desire in a housing style. For example, an Italianate Mediterranean-style home will incorporate elements evident in the work of esteemed architect Andrea Palladio and the Renaissance work of Michelangelo. When researching a style, he generates concepts and designs plans with attention given

LEFT:
Classical forms are arranged to create exterior rooms.
Photograph by Tom Raymond, Fresh Air Photographics

to how one moves through the space, determining circulation patterns and connecting rooms to create a "design overlay" atop the client's preferences.

Sites are carefully analyzed, each home designed relative to its context. Whether the residence is situated in a suburban gated golf community, on an equestrian property, country estate, lakeside location or in the highlands, making the home livable for today and taking advantage of the site is of utmost importance. Classical architectural concepts and theories are applied to each home and room arrangements are made fresh and contemporized, albeit relatively traditional. In one residential project, the historically classical "great hall" was uniquely incorporated around a sunken courtyard space to achieve a smooth and fluid circulation flow. Each home is strategically designed to receive natural light and capture its beautiful interplay with form to create a remarkable experience upon entering the space. Reflecting this design aesthetic, many respected clients have given the highest of compliments, stating: "Our home feels like a church."

Being a small firm allows the studio to focus on a handful of select projects each year, including new custom constructions, additions and adaptive use renovations. Working foremost in Atlanta, the firm

TOP LEFT:
While interesting in its own right, the sunken entry courtyard draws attention to the spectacular architecture.
Photograph by Tom Raymond, Fresh Air Photographics

BOTTOM LEFT:
Multi-tone paneling provides lightness for the rich bedroom.
Photograph by Tom Raymond, Fresh Air Photographics

FACING PAGE:
With its classical beams and purlin ceiling system, this is the return of the great hall as a living space.
Photograph by Tom Raymond, Fresh Air Photographics

also designs custom residences in Nashville's equestrian communities and throughout Tennessee and Alabama. Designing for a diverse clientele, Jim designs specifically for each client's unique program of needs; building around lifestyle preferences to express who they truly are. He asks probing questions to help discern how to best accommodate present day needs and those well into the future.

The firm's scope ranges from designing a modern addition for a 1930s' vintage home to a spacious Tuscan-inspired farmhouse; a multi-family, mid-rise institutional building, commercial space or historic adaptive-use project. Jim consistently explores historical precedence and its detailed methodology, yet his work most exemplifies contemporary architectural theory emphasizing the "now." His studio is located near Dr. Martin Luther King Jr.'s renowned Ebenezer Baptist Church in a revitalized historic district of Atlanta, reinforcing his love for "walking cities" and appreciation for urban density. Living with his wife and family in a rare Victorian residence amid yet another historic Atlanta neighborhood, Jim is immersed in and inspired by great architecture, which informs his work every day.

WILSON & DAWSON ARCHITECTS
Jim Wilson
417 Edgewood Avenue
Atlanta, GA 30312
404.522.2142
f: 404.522.2143
www.wilson-dawson.com

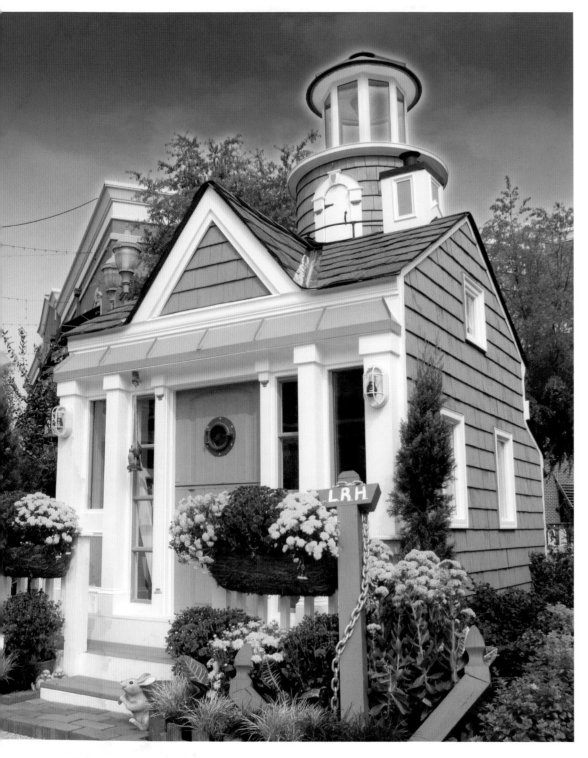

ABOVE:
The "Spirit of Light" playhouse was designed by Garrell Associates and built by Lanier Resort Homes. This is a detailed replica of the St. Simons Lighthouse, a seaside historic landmark in St. Simons Island, Georgia.
Photograph by Warren Bond

ABOVE:
The "Kidz Court" playhouse was designed by Garrell Associates and built by Country Classic Builders. The replica building was fashioned after the Fayette County Courthouse from 1825—the oldest courthouse in Georgia located in Fayetteville.
Photograph by Warren Bond

HomeAid
Atlanta

HomeAid's **Project Playhouse™**

HOMEAID ATLANTA
Project Playhouse

Project Playhouse™ is much more than child's play—it is a heartfelt community service project and signature fundraiser to benefit those people in metro Atlanta who are temporarily homeless.

Every year Atlanta's most talented and generous architects and home builders, along with their building partners, work together to create fantasy playhouses that delight young and old alike. Offering their time and materials, using superior craftsmanship, imagination and inspired by architectural historic precedence, they build miniature replica homes and original, whimsical designs. Each playhouse is completely furnished and has the latest electronics as well as children's books and fun games to fulfill the dreams of any child.

These child-size showcase homes are donated, displayed for public viewing and sold at a festive annual auction to raise money benefiting HomeAid Atlanta. Recognition awards are given to the building partners in various categories including the Craftsman Award, Imagination Award, Rainbow Award, Mirror Image Award, Secret Garden Award and Neel Reid Award.

It is a distinguishing honor to be recognized as a Project Playhouse™ participant and a joy for those who are fortunate to have the highest bid.

The mission of HomeAid Atlanta, the charity of the Greater Atlanta Home Builders Association, is to build dignified, transitional housing where homeless families and individuals can rebuild their lives. This is accomplished through the donation of construction services and materials from members of the homebuilding industry.

Information about HomeAid Atlanta and its projects and events can be found on the organization's Web site.

HOMEAID ATLANTA
Ann Carey
1484 Brockett Road
Tucker, GA 30084
678.775.1401
f: 770.934.8363
www.homeaidatlanta.org

PUBLISHING TEAM

Brian G. Carabet, Publisher
John A. Shand, Publisher
Phil Reavis, Executive Publisher
Janet Smiley, Associate Publisher

Beth Benton, Director of Development & Design
Elizabeth Gionta, Editorial Development
Julia Hoover, Director of Book Marketing & Distribution

Michele Cunningham-Scott, Art Director
Mary Elizabeth Acree, Graphic Designer
Emily Kattan, Graphic Designer
Ben Quintanilla, Graphic Designer

Rosalie Z. Wilson, Managing Editor
Lauren Castelli, Editor
Anita M. Kasmar, Editor
Ryan Parr, Editor

Kristy Randall, Lead Production Coordinator
Laura Greenwood, Production Coordinator
Jennifer Lenhart, Production Coordinator
Jessica Garrison, Traffic Coordinator

Carol Kendall, Project Manager
Beverly Smith, Project Manager

PANACHE PARTNERS, LLC
CORPORATE OFFICE
13747 Montfort Drive, Suite 100
Dallas, TX 75240
972.661.9884
www.panache.com

GEORGIA OFFICE
Janet Smiley 678.557.2754

Zoran Design Associates, page 229

THE PANACHE COLLECTION

Dream Homes Series

Dream Homes of Texas
Dream Homes South Florida
Dream Homes Colorado
Dream Homes Metro New York
Dream Homes Greater Philadelphia
Dream Homes New Jersey
Dream Homes Florida
Dream Homes Southwest
Dream Homes Northern California
Dream Homes the Carolinas
Dream Homes Georgia
Dream Homes Chicago
Dream Homes San Diego & Orange County
Dream Homes Washington, D.C.
Dream Homes Deserts
Dream Homes Pacific Northwest
Dream Homes Minnesota
Dream Homes Ohio & Pennsylvania
Dream Homes California Central Coast
Dream Homes Connecticut
Dream Homes Los Angeles
Dream Homes Michigan
Dream Homes Tennessee
Dream Homes New England

Additional Titles

Spectacular Hotels
Spectacular Golf of Texas
Spectacular Golf of Colorado
Spectacular Restaurants of Texas
Elite Portfolios
Spectacular Wineries of Napa Valley

City by Design Series

City by Design Dallas
City by Design Atlanta
City by Design San Francisco Bay Area
City by Design Pittsburgh
City by Design Chicago
City by Design Charlotte
City by Design Phoenix, Tucson & Albuquerque
City by Design Denver

Perspectives on Design Series

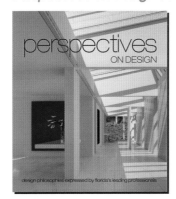

Perspectives on Design Florida

Spectacular Homes Series

Spectacular Homes of Texas
Spectacular Homes of Georgia
Spectacular Homes of South Florida
Spectacular Homes of Tennessee
Spectacular Homes of the Pacific Northwest
Spectacular Homes of Greater Philadelphia
Spectacular Homes of the Southwest
Spectacular Homes of Colorado
Spectacular Homes of the Carolinas
Spectacular Homes of Florida
Spectacular Homes of California
Spectacular Homes of Michigan
Spectacular Homes of the Heartland
Spectacular Homes of Chicago
Spectacular Homes of Washington, D.C.
Spectacular Homes of Ohio & Pennsylvania
Spectacular Homes of Minnesota
Spectacular Homes of New England
Spectacular Homes of New York

Visit www.panache.com or call
972.661.9884

PANACHE PARTNERS, LLC

Creators of Spectacular Publications for
Discerning Readers

INDEX

PFVS Architects, Inc., page 259

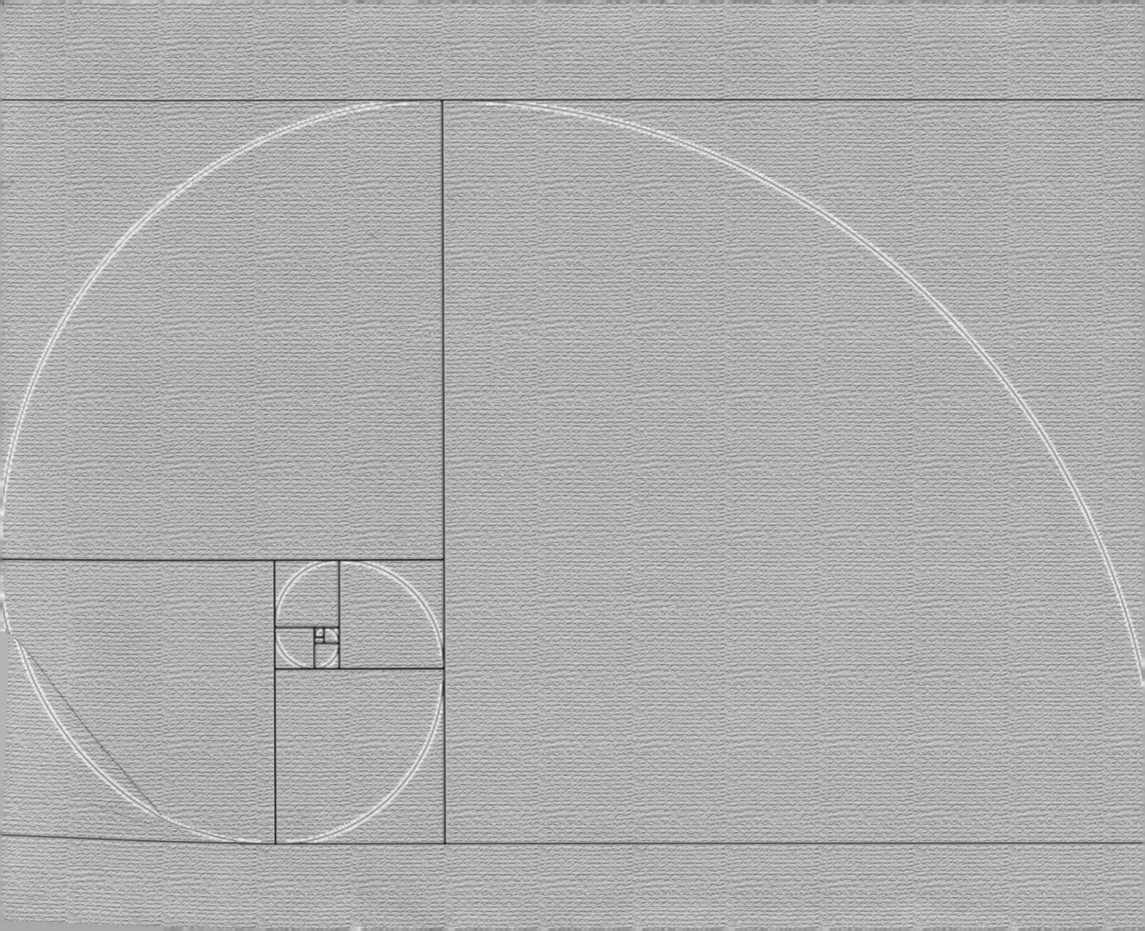